"Casey has solved the what-to-bring problem delightfully and deliciously. All that's left to us is the fun of turning up at someone's door with dishes they'll love."
—**DORIE GREENSPAN**, author of *Baking with Dorie*

"*What Can I Bring?* seriously brings the party. Each recipe gets me more excited than the last, and I can't wait to cook everything!"
—**JUSTINE DOIRON**, author of *Justine Cooks*

"*What Can I Bring?* is overflowing with irresistible, easy-to-make dishes that scream "party hero." Get ready to impress, indulge, and live your best guest life!"
—**ANDY BARAGHANI**, author of *The Cook You Want to Be*

"An invitation to relax with friends should be cause for excitement, not stress, and luckily, we have the talented and openhearted Casey with delicious solutions for every scenario!"
—**NATASHA LI PICKOWICZ**, author of *More Than Cake*

"*What Can I Bring?* is your new go-to for perfect cocktails, elevated salads, best-ever dinner rolls (hello, Thanksgiving!), and crazy-good cakes. Casey has the ideal recipe for every occasion!"
—**TIEGHAN GERARD**, author of *Half Baked Harvest Quick & Cozy*

"*What Can I Bring?* is a gorgeous guide to winning 'best party guest'! Casey knows exactly what to bring for every occasion, with approachable, sophisticated recipes."
—**RICK MARTÍNEZ,** author of *Mi Cocina*

# What Can
I Bring?

## CASEY ELSASS

# WHAT CAN I BRING?

## Recipes to Help You Live Your Guest Life

Photographs by Gentl and Hyers

U

UNION
SQUARE
& CO.

NEW YORK

UNION
SQUARE
& CO.

NEW YORK

ISBN 978-1-4549-5534-4
ISBN 978-1-4549-5535-1 (e-book)

For information about custom editions, special sales,
and premium purchases, please contact specialsales@
unionsquareandco.com.

Printed in China

10 9 8 7 6 5 4 3 2 1

unionsquareandco.com

Editor: Caitlin Leffel
Designer: Renée Bollier
Photographers: Gentl and Hyers
Food Stylist: Tyna Hoang
Prop Stylist: Stephanie De Luca
Project Editor: Ivy McFadden
Production Manager: Terence Campo
Copy Editor: Terry Deal

To getting
together

If you're always on time,
bring appetizers.

If you're reliably late,
bring a drink.

If you're stopping
by later, bring dessert.

If you're bringing
nothing else,
bring a present.

# INTRODUCTION

# WHAT CAN I BRING?

**IT'S THE FIRST QUESTION** everyone asks when you get *the invite*.

Okay, maybe the first question is "What time?" or "Who all will be there?" or "Can I bring my partner/spouse/lover/side piece?" But every polite guest has to ask the big one eventually, and no other question has such high stakes and personal consequences. That's Problem #1.

Once you've been asked to bring something, we get to Problem #2: Bringing a dish to a party is definitely not a competition, but it also kind of is? Everyone secretly wants to be *the* dish that gets second helpings, whispers of "Did you try that?!," and polished off first. Who among us doesn't want to bask in the warm glow of that praise?

Social gatherings used to be so easy. All you had to do was strap on multiple constrictive layers, climb the ranks of society, master the art of small talk, and know which of twenty-four utensils to use when. A breeze! Today, we have to navigate very casual dinner parties, cookouts, backyard hangs, holiday gatherings, and movie nights, so the English language led us to four loaded words: "What can I bring?"

*What Can I Bring?* (that's the name of this book, we're not circling back to Problem #1) is bypassing the $12 bottle of pinot grigio and encouraging you to share your culinary gifts with all the addictive dips, fun little drinks, and unreal desserts (two chapters' worth!) you could ever possibly want. You'll have the ideal salad that's not only easy to pack up and transport, but will stand out in the crowd. An impressive brunch dish can be prepped the night before so you'll arrive with an effortless air! If you're still rattled from your failed sourdough attempts, there are plenty of breads to get you back on track at a wide range of skill levels. And for those lucky moments when the host tells you to just bring yourself, a short chapter of giftable edible treats will make sure you get invited back ASAP. Think of this book as seventy-five perfect, anxiety-free answers you can offer to bring when it's time to ask the big question.

Oops, sorry, I totally jumped right into problem-solving and forgot to introduce myself. I'm Casey Elsass, and this is my book. I write cookbooks and develop recipes for a living (yes, it's a dream job), so I spend most of my days cooking, eating, thinking, writing, and talking about food. I also lead a busy social life and, not to brag, I get invited to a lot of things. I also—sorry, truly not bragging—get invited *back* to a lot of things. What I'm saying is A) I've been bringing stuff places for years, and B) I know how to make delicious food.

But most importantly, I want to say: I am not a foodie—I am someone who loves food. And by that I mean I genuinely love *all* food in all its forms. I don't believe in looking down or judging or calling things "high-low." I've had flush years and I've had tight years, and I appreciate that we all come to the kitchen from different economic standings and geographic access to food. I cook from the principle that anything you can get your hands on can become something extraordinary, and I hope everyone feels welcome to find joy and excitement in these pages.

I'm also deeply curious and excited about food, and I'm lucky to live in a city that fuels my curiosity with infinite cultures and perspectives. When I travel to a new country, all I want to do is walk through a grocery store and touch everything, go everywhere, and eat everything, and then come home and infuse all that into my own cooking. I love to play with flavors and ideas and encourage everyone to do the same, because curiosity, play, and learning are one and the same. But part of learning has to be knowing where your food comes from, in every sense, and I've tried to acknowledge history and traditions where I can. My mind and stomach are hungry all the time, and I'm always eager to learn more, expand my horizons, and fall deeper in love with food.

So, basically, I hope you'll see this book as much more than seventy-five recipes rescuing you from a total meltdown, because secretly, it's also a loving guide from one home cook with a lot of experience (that's me) to a lot of home cooks with various levels of experience (that's you, plural). The point of a cookbook is to instruct and educate, so I want to meet you wherever you are on your journey of comfort in the kitchen and help you learn to cook smarter, build confidence, get your creative juices flowing, and feel ownership over your own set of go-to recipes.

I also hope you won't feel limited to making these recipes *only* on a to-bring basis. Almost everything in here would fit right in as an element for your own weeknight meal, a snacky lunch, or—twist!—when you're the one hosting and need to lay out a perfect spread. I think every dish needs a good test run before it's introduced to the public, anyway, so give it a whirl for yourself first!

*What Can I Bring?* is packed with the things I genuinely love to make and my specific ways of making them, tested over years and years of successes and failures. And now they're your set of forever recipes to nail and tweak as you make them over and over and over. So next time you ask your friend "What can I bring?" I hope your heart will start racing with excitement at all the possibilities waiting on the other side of their reply.

# Live Your Guest Life

It's not just important to bring the right thing. It's equally—if not more!—important to be the kind of guest everyone loves to have around. Here are a few simple rules that, in my opinion, will make you not just a good guest but a great one.

→ **be honest about what kind of guest you are**

If you missed it on the Contents page, I'll say it again: If you're always on time, bring appetizers. If you're reliably late, bring a drink. If you're stopping by later, bring dessert. If you're bringing nothing else, bring a present. Make sure you're committing to a dish that matches your dillydallying or extremely punctual self.

→ **embrace room-temp food**

The best guests show up with a dish that's ready to go without needing a shelf in the fridge or a rack in the oven. Some recipes here are exceptions to this rule, and for those (or anything else), just clear it with your host ahead of time so they're in on the plan. *Never* show up expecting to derail their careful game of culinary Tetris for something of your own.

→ **come prepared**

Besides having your food ready to go, make sure you pack everything you need. Their home is not your Williams Sonoma. Serving utensils, a big bowl, or special cups are your responsibility. For common things, like a knife to cut the cake, just ask ahead of time so you know you're covered.

→ **be kind**

The recipes are labeled with dietary info (we'll get to that in a sec) so you can be kind to your fellow guests. If you know other people are gluten sensitive or have a nut allergy or are three weeks into going vegan, see if there's something that sounds good *and* works for them. It's a really nice gesture, and they'll never forget it. But also be kind to yourself! The recipes are labeled with effort level (again, I'll cover that in a moment), so pick something that matches the amount of work you're willing to put in right now. Do not overextend yourself—you'll just feel miserable and self-conscious. Make what you want to make!

## → bring a disposable camera

This is a little more event-specific. For example, a quiet, intimate dinner party might not be the right time. (And it might not *not* be the right time—trust your gut.) But every birthday, backyard, cocktail, surprise, holiday, pool, and house-warming party absolutely needs an analog presence. Make it known that there's a camera up for grabs and let everyone go nuts. The huge element of mystery makes it 1,000% more fun than phone pictures. Develop the pictures digitally and send a download link to the other guests so you can all relive the night a week later.

## → say thank you

My friends Kyle Marshall and Julia Bainbridge are two of the most naturally elegant people I know. I once had Kyle over for a group dinner and Julia over for a small brunch. Two business days later, there was a card sitting in my mailbox simply saying thank you. It's a small but impactful gesture. Don't be awkward and send your besties an earnest card (mail them the most inappropriate Hallmark card you can find), but if you're new friends with someone or it was a very important event, a thank-you card is an old-fashioned gesture that still lands in this century. Even if a card isn't right for the occasion, a simple text goes a long way to making your host feel seen and appreciated.

# Tips Before You Start

Before you dive into the recipes, I want to share some global cooking notes that I've adopted over the years. If you want to make sure you nail it every time, here's what you need to know.

**the great salt debate**

Everyone has their go-to salt and—lol, of course—every salt is totally different. Table salt, sea salt, and kosher salt have diverse grain sizes, varying levels of saltiness, and different melting points. I buy big bulk boxes of Diamond Crystal kosher salt, which is on the more expensive side. If you prefer Morton kosher salt, or you like the taste of a fine sea salt, or you're faithful to Himalayan pink salt, or you're a tried-and-true table salt household, just cut the listed salt amount in half. (For example, ½ teaspoon kosher salt for me would be ¼ teaspoon of your preferred salt for you.) A big flaky salt, like Maldon or Jacobsen, is meant for garnish and won't get you far in cooking. Anything flavored, like smoked salt or sulfuric black salt, is for specific uses only.

**building flavor**

Taste early and taste often. Everything in this book is based on what tastes good to me. Maybe we'll agree on that and maybe we won't, so it's your job to sneak little nibbles while cooking to make sure it's feeling great to you. I like to build flavor with layers of spices, herbs, acids, and fats, and each element is going to adjust the overall experience. Tasting along the way will help build an understanding of how each ingredient contributes to the bigger picture, plus a database of your own preferences and customizations.

**engage your senses**

Cooking is not a race, so don't just plow through the recipe. Chill out and stay present. Use all five senses to confirm that everything is going to plan. Taste, sight, smell, sound, and feel all have to work together when you're in the kitchen, and using them is the fastest way to become a more intuitive cook. Does that sizzle sound dreamy? Is the cake golden brown? Can you smell the spices? Do the veggies feel soft? Constant check-ins will keep you from going off the rails, and smart problem solving will bring anything back from the brink.

## the holy trinity

I think every kitchen needs three things: a kitchen timer, an oven thermometer, and a comically large mixing bowl. You'll notice every recipe in this book says "set a timer for X minutes." That's because I don't trust myself to not get distracted, and (I'm so sorry to say this) I don't trust you either. So keep a kitchen timer nearby! I have a windup Zassenhaus that magnetically sticks to my fridge, and I use the timer setting on my microwave if I need a second countdown. I don't use my phone because the moment I touch that thing, I get distracted and forget everything. Next up, my oven. I have a grumpy old New York apartment gas oven that views temperature as more of a suggestion than a rule. But even new ovens can have wild inaccuracies in temperature—sometimes by as much as 50 degrees! So when you turn on your oven to preheat, set a thermometer as close to the center of the oven as possible. After adjusting and confirming I'm at the right temp, I take the thermometer out and slide my goodies in, an easy way to make sure I'm right on target. And finally, the bowl. I'm talking big, like "where in the world am I going to put this bowl?" kind of big. Eight quarts is my preferred size (but make sure you *can* actually put that somewhere) when I need to mix, toss, soak, marinate, make an ice bath, or proof dough without worrying about running out of space or spilling over the edges.

## weigh in

If you want to get serious about baking, buy a kitchen scale. King Arthur says 1 cup of all-purpose flour is 120 grams, America's Test Kitchen says it's 142 grams, I've asked friends to weigh a scoop for me and they've been anywhere from 130 grams to over 150 grams. You see the problem? All the baking recipes in this book have a weight in grams listed next to anything over ¼ cup for accuracy. They were developed and tested by weight first and later double checked by volume, but the best way I can ensure accuracy with my recipes, or anyone else's for that matter, is if you break out the scale. It's going to feel clunky at first until you get into a rhythm with the tare button, which sets the scale back to zero after you weigh each ingredient. It's especially great for sticky and saucy things, which you can just pour directly into the mixing bowl and bypass washing a measuring cup! And for the record, I think a cup of flour is 140 grams and I won't be taking questions at this time.

## clean as you go

Here is the number one thing that made me forever fall in love with cooking: learning to clean as I work. An uncluttered and clean workspace will do more for your mental health than anything else. Before you do any prep, start by wiping down your counters, scrubbing your sink, and washing your hands thoroughly. Then do your best to keep those three things as clean as possible. I always set out a plate so any spatulas, spoons, or whisks can rest there instead of the counter. I keep a kitchen towel around to swipe up

spills. Any little prep bowls go straight to the sink as soon as I empty them, and I wash them the second I have some down time. (This is exactly why I need the timer!) When you get to the end of a recipe and the dishes are already done, you will feel absolutely unstoppable.

**presentation is everything**

If you're going to put real effort into your cooking, make sure it looks as good as it tastes. I've tried to give you a head start with lots of colors, textures, and garnishes, but the rest is up to you. Use a bowl or plate that lets the food shine while making it look bountiful, give a salad a little fluff so it has plenty of height, swirl a spoon on the dip so the texture looks irresistible, swoop that spatula until the frosting is photo ready, make sure the garnishes go on just before serving so they're super fresh, and there's no shame in a shower of fresh parsley or colorful sprinkles to hide imperfections.

# How Does This Work?

To help make this book easy and digestible, every recipe is broken down into specific elements, noted in the handy example to the right. Do me a **HUGE** favor and read every part of the recipe *before* you start. No, I'm serious. Read it all the way through. Check if there are long gaps to let something chill or rise. Be sure you don't need to order any ingredients or equipment online. Imagine each step of the process, thinking about where you're going and how you're going to get there. Let me walk you through what you'll see on each recipe page:

A. When someone asks, "Oooo what is this?," here is your answer.

B. A secret little code just for us so you know how much effort each recipe requires. *In Your Sleep* means a super easy recipe, barely any effort required. *Roll Up Your Sleeves* means there's some work involved here, but you'll breeze right through it. *Bragging Rights* means I need your head in the game, but we're going to nail this together. Notice how I didn't use any words like "hard," "a challenge," or "sobbing on the floor of your kitchen"? That's because all of these recipes were designed to be easy, approachable, guaranteed hits.

C. Each recipe will let you know if it's vegan, vegetarian, gluten-free, nut-free, or a combo of those things, and drinks will also let you know if they're nonalcoholic. If anything shows up in parentheses, it means that with a very easy substitution, it can bend to that dietary restriction.

D. Some background info on the recipe so you know what you're getting into, plus any cute tidbits you can share when you serve it to others.

E. The serving size, so you can be sure there's plenty for everyone.

F. Your grocery list. Some things might need some light prep ahead of time, like chopping onions or softening butter. If the prep is a little more specific or can happen while cooking, it'll be noted for you in the recipe instead.

G. If you like to cook, I'm going to assume you have measuring cups, knives, and a trusty rubber spatula. This is anything extra that your kitchen might not necessarily have.

H. The recipe itself! I want you to feel like we're in this together, so I'll be explaining the how and why as we go. I'm constantly absorbing new info as a cook, so no matter how experienced you are, I hope there will be fresh insight here for you.

I. In the interest of keeping the recipe moving, I've included some footnotes at the bottom with important intel, easy substitutions, or instructions for packing everything up.

Okay, enough yapping, let's get cooking!

A

# Spiced Hibiscus Punch

B
C

IN YOUR SLEEP | V, GF, NF, NA

D

We're all grown-ups here, so there is no excuse for a boring bowl of punch. Even without alcohol, this is as far from a school dance as it can possibly be. Hibiscus flowers (you might be familiar with their work in agua de jamaica or Red Zinger tea bags) have a kind of cranberry tartness that pairs really well with mulling spices and citrus. Find the spiciest ginger beer (not ginger ale, we're leaving the past behind) you can for a bubbly, burning background to your fruity party drink. Balancing a floating ring of decorative ice in the bowl is the perfect cinematic final touch.

E

**Makes 11 cups, enough for 15 people**

F

1 cup dried hibiscus flowers
    (see Party Tricks)
1 cup sugar
4 thyme sprigs
2 cinnamon sticks
6 star anise pods
¾ cup fresh grapefruit juice
    (from 1 grapefruit)
¼ cup fresh lime juice (from 2 to
    3 limes)
4 (12-ounce) bottles extra-
    strong ginger beer of your
    choice
1 (12-ounce) can seltzer
Ice ring (see Party Tricks), for
    serving

G

**SPECIAL EQUIPMENT**
3-quart punch bowl and
    decorative ladle
Plastic tumblers or punch cups

In a large saucepan, combine the hibiscus, sugar, thyme, cinnamon, star anise, and 3 cups water. Bring to a boil over high heat, then reduce to the lowest possible heat, cover, and set a timer for 30 minutes. When the timer goes off, remove from the heat and strain the liquid into a large punch bowl. Cool completely, about 1 hour.

H

Add the grapefruit juice and lime juice to the bowl and just before serving, pour in the ginger beer and seltzer. Add the ice ring, drop in the ladle, set out the cups, and let everyone serve themselves.

**PARTY TRICKS**

I

- Hibiscus flowers can be found online or in a Mexican grocery. Hibiscus tea bags will also work in a pinch; use 8 so the tea is strong.

- If you're making this to go, strain the hibiscus tea into an airtight container and refrigerate for up to 3 days. Add the grapefruit and lime juices to the container just before leaving, and pack the bowl, ice ring, ginger beer, and seltzer to assemble on arrival.

**V = Vegan**
**VG = Vegetarian**
**GF = Gluten-Free**
**NF = Nut-Free**
**NA = Nonalcoholic**

**In Your Sleep = Super Easy**
**Roll Up Your Sleeves = Some Effort**
**Bragging Rights = Extra Focus**

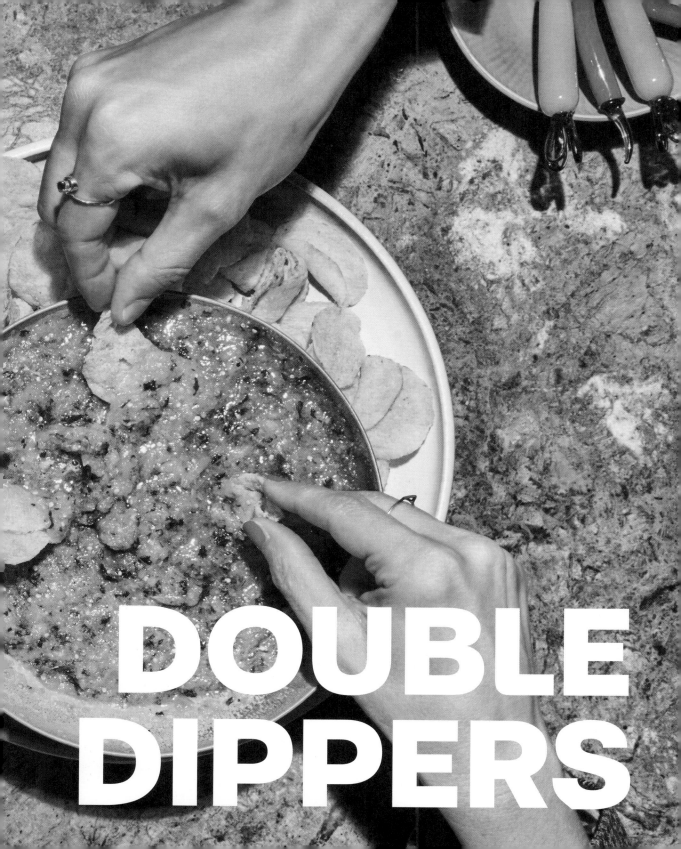

# DOUBLE
# DIPPERS

**THERE'S NO BETTER WAY** to start a party (or a book about parties) than laying out a solid group of dips. This chapter has some forever-classics with fail-proof methods, plus some new staples to expand your repertoire. Dips are perfect snacky, social foods—by nature, meant to be shared. They're also great conversation starters. For example: *Did you try that one? It's from What Can I Bring? by Casey Elsass. Have you read it?*

# Golden Ratio Guac

There are a million correct ways to make guac and I would like to eat all of them, thank you. But when I'm in the driver's seat, this is how I do it. The key is an obsessive level of chopping, getting everything fine, fine, fine so the aromatics beautifully coat the avocado and every bite is *consistent*. (If only we all had an inherited molcajete in our kitchens to speed this up, but most of us aren't that lucky.) If you want a guac that stands out from the crowd, follow along!

**Makes 3 cups, enough for 4 to 6 people**

¼ white onion
1 jalapeño
1 garlic clove
1 medium lime (keep a second one handy just in case)
½ cup loosely packed fresh cilantro leaves and stems
1 teaspoon kosher salt
½ teaspoon ground cumin (optional, but highly recommended)
⅛ teaspoon sodium bisulfite (see Party Tricks; optional)
4 large ripe avocados (see Party Tricks)
Nonstick cooking spray
Tortilla chips, for serving

Dice the onion, then run your knife over it a few more times to finely chop. Right on top of the onion, cut the jalapeño into thin rounds, then dice. (I think the seeds are fine here for a very manageable spice level, but you can remove them. See Party Tricks on page 35 for an easy hack.) Grate the garlic and zest the lime on top of the onion jalapeño mixture. Chop the mixture, running your knife back and forth, then scraping everything into the center of the board, chopping, and scraping, back and forth, until it's almost like a paste. Lay the cilantro on top and chop into uneven but smallish pieces. I know this all seems like a lot of work, but we're making a seasoning paste that's going to guarantee an even distribution of flavor throughout the guac.

Lift up the cutting board and use the *back* of the knife blade to scrape everything into a medium bowl, really dragging on the board to get all that good flavor out. Roll the zested lime with your palm to release the juices. Cut it in half and squeeze it into the bowl. Add the salt, cumin, and sodium bisulfate, if you're going down that path, and use a wire whisk to lightly mix everything together.

Cut the avocados in half, remove the pits, and use a spoon to scoop the flesh into the bowl. Use the whisk again to smash and stir the avocados—the firm wires on a whisk are the perfect tool for the kind of irregular mashing I love in my guac. Make sure to leave some larger chunks of avocado while moving the seasonings around. Take a taste. I might add another ¼ teaspoon of salt, maybe call in that second lime. Remember, tortilla chips are salty, so trying a bite in situ is always a good idea. At this point, switch to a spoon to stir since the whisk will only continue to break up the avocado.

*Recipe continues*

Scrape the guac into a medium bowl. Lightly (LIGHTLY!) spritz a piece of parchment with nonstick spray and press it on top and around the edges of the guac so the entire surface is covered. Guac is really meant to be served at room temperature—it allows the fatty avocado flavor to sing—so make this right before go time and don't refrigerate. Give it a good stir just before serving and set out plenty of tortilla chips for dipping.

## PARTY TRICKS

- Lime juice, avocado pits, blah blah blah. If you want your guac to stay perfectly green for hours, there's only one surefire way: a chemical assist. A little wonder called sodium bisulfite blocks the oxidation that causes guac to go grayish-brown. It is a preservative, I won't lie to you, but it's used in a lot of foods. It's totally your call, but the small amount here is pretty harmless and will keep your dip looking shockingly fresh. I get mine from Kalustyan's (foodsofnations.com), which ships nationally.

- Landing a ripe avocado can sometimes feel like a fool's errand. In the store, avoid light green skin (too firm) and black skin (too mushy) and look for skin that's a rich dark green (just right). But in reality, the safest bet when it comes to avocados is to buy ahead. Four days before, I'll buy the lightest green ones that are totally firm all over and set them out on my counter. Around day 2 or 3, they'll be ripe and at that point they can be held in the refrigerator for another day or two. Just bring them to room temp before using.

*Seven-Onion Dip, 28*

*Cornmeal Crackers, 123*

# Faux Gras

*Optional: Start this recipe 1 day ahead.*

If you're like me and you feel iffy about liver pâté—I've had great ones and I've had stomach churners—then this little science project has your name written all over it. It's a laundry list of ingredients that all play an important role: soaked cashews for heft, dried shiitake and miso for umami, tomato paste for color, molasses for minerality, cornstarch and xanthan gum for coagulation, Cognac for a very classic foie gras flavor profile, and Crisco for a fatty richness. It's a little pantry alchemy, and I can't get enough.

**Makes 2 cups, enough for 8 people**

½ cup raw cashews
4 tablespoons vegetable shortening, such as Crisco
6 dried shiitake mushrooms
1 medium shallot, thinly sliced
1 garlic clove, thinly sliced
¼ cup plus 1 tablespoon Cognac or brandy (see Party Tricks)
2 tablespoons white miso paste
1 tablespoon tomato paste
2 tablespoons unsulfured molasses
½ teaspoon kosher salt
½ teaspoon freshly ground black pepper
½ teaspoon Chinese five-spice (see Party Trick on page 167; optional, but highly recommended)
1 teaspoon cornstarch
½ teaspoon xanthan gum (see Party Tricks)
Your favorite crackers or bread or Cornmeal Crackers (page 123), for serving

Combine the cashews and 2 cups cold water in a 1-pint jar or other airtight container. Refrigerate to soak for at least 2 hours or up to overnight.

Drain the cashews and keep them nearby. Get your blender out and at the ready. In a small saucepan, melt 1 tablespoon of the shortening over low heat. Add the mushrooms, shallot, and garlic. Cook, stirring occasionally, until the shallot is starting to get soft, about 3 minutes. Add the cashews and Cognac, cover, and set a timer for 4 minutes. This will let everything hydrate and some of the liquid reduce.

When the timer goes off, remove the lid and stir in the miso, tomato, paste, molasses, salt, pepper, five-spice, and 1 tablespoon of the shortening. Add ½ cup water and increase the heat to high. When the mixture is at a rapid boil, immediately pour it into the blender with the remaining 1 tablespoon Cognac. Tilt the blender lid so there's an air vent and start blending on low, working up to high speed. Stop to scrape down the sides and add 1 tablespoon water along with the cornstarch and xanthan gum. Start on low and work up to high, blending until everything is incorporated and thick, about 1 minute.

Scrape the mixture into a wide-mouth pint jar or small serving bowl. Melt the remaining 2 tablespoons shortening and pour over top of the faux gras. Screw the lid on and refrigerate for at least 1 hour or up to 4 days to set the pâté. Remove from the fridge and let stand at room temperature for 30 minutes before serving.

## PARTY TRICKS

- If you want to make this alcohol-free, use 2 tablespoons of apple juice for a similarly fruity note.

- You'll find xanthan gum hanging out in the baking aisle or the gluten-free section. Bob's Red Mill makes it and is commonly found in most grocery stores.

# Seven-Onion Dip

ROLL UP YOUR SLEEVES | VG, GF, NF (V)

Technically it's seven members of the onion *family*, but it's a catchy name, right? Shallots, leeks, scallions, chives, garlic, and anything with the word onion are all branches of the Allium family tree, which is why they all share a similarly sharp and pungent flavor. And that is why this family reunion makes for the most incredible bowl of onion dip you've ever had.

*(Pictured on page 25)*

**Makes 4 cups, enough for 8 people**

2 tablespoons extra-virgin olive oil
4 tablespoons unsalted butter
1 medium Vidalia, Spanish, or yellow onion
1 medium red onion
4 medium shallots
2 large leeks
1 tablespoon sugar
1 tablespoon tamari, soy sauce, or fish sauce (see Party Tricks)
1 teaspoon kosher salt
8 scallions
1 bunch chives
6 garlic cloves
1 (8-ounce) block cream cheese
1 cup sour cream
½ cup mayonnaise
1 teaspoon freshly ground black pepper
A pinch of cayenne pepper (optional)
Has to be Ruffles, for serving

Swirl the olive oil to coat the bottom of a large saucepan and set the butter in the center. Keep it on the counter to hold all the chopping we're about to do.

Trim the stem and root end off of the Vidalia onion, cut it in half, and peel the skin off. Place each half cut side down, thinly slice across, then scoop the slices into the saucepan. Do the same with the red onion and shallots. Wash the leeks under cold water to rinse off any dirt or sand from the outside. Trim the dark green tops off the leeks, then run the knife from root to tip to cut them in half. Hold the leek halves root side up and rinse the insides under cold water again, using your thumbs to spread the layers and let any dirt wash out. Set the halves cut side down, thinly slice across, and add to the saucepan. Dry off the cutting board and keep it nearby.

Set the saucepan over medium heat and use a wooden spoon to stir the onions a little as the butter melts. As the onions start to sizzle, stir frequently to prevent sticking. After about 10 minutes, they should start to look pretty soft. Stir in the sugar, tamari, salt, 2 tablespoons water and reduce the heat to low. (If you have an open bottle of white wine laying around anyway, use it instead of the water.) Set a timer for 30 minutes, checking in and giving your babies a stir every 10 minutes or so, until the onions are nicely caramelized and jammy.

While the onions are going, finish your knife work. Trim the roots off the scallions, thinly slice all the way up, and slide them to one side of the board. Thinly slice the chives and slide that pile to the other side.

When the timer goes off, scoop up half the scallions and half the chives and drop them into the onion mixture. Grate the garlic directly into the saucepan. Stir everything together, make a judgment call if it needs another tablespoon of water—or another sip of wine—and cook for 5 more minutes, until the scallions are soft and the garlic is super fragrant. Remove from the stove and nestle the cream cheese brick in the center of the saucepan. Set a timer for 30 minutes and leave it alone to cool down.

When the timer goes off, use a rubber spatula to scrape the cream cheese and onions into a food processor. Add in the sour cream, mayonnaise, black pepper, and a teensy pinch of cayenne, if you want. Process for about 2 minutes, stopping to scrape down the sides halfway, until you have a blended dip with a little bit of texture. Scrape the dip into a medium bowl and fold in the reserved scallions and chives. Cover tightly with plastic wrap and refrigerate. This should really be made 1 or 2 days before so the flavors have plenty of time to marry, but 4 hours will also do the trick. Let the dip sit at room temperature for at least 30 minutes before serving with Ruffles, no exceptions. I'm so sorry to all other chips.

## PARTY TRICKS

- Look for leeks that have majority white/light green stalks and minimal dark green tops, which are too rough to use. Or just buy an extra leek to make up the difference.

- Quickly: Tamari is vegan and gluten-free, soy sauce is vegan but has gluten, and fish sauce is obviously not vegan and sometimes (but not always) has gluten. Pick your poison!

- To make this vegan, grab your favorite brands of vegan cream cheese, sour cream, and mayo and go to town.

# Silky Hummus

ROLL UP YOUR SLEEVES | V, GF, NF

**When you've experienced hummus freshly made in a restaurant that is *so serious* about their hummus, it's really hard to feel okay about store-bought. I know that's such an annoying thing to say, but, unfortunately, it's the truth. It's lighter, airier, softer, and more addictive than a packaged brand could ever achieve. The good news is you can make excellent hummus of your own—in a food processor! with canned chickpeas!—and even though there are some steps to follow, nothing about it is *hard*. It's perfect on its own, or you can follow my advice for crunchy, spicy, or herby toppings to boost it even more.**

**Makes 2½ cups, enough for 6 people**

3 tablespoons fresh lemon juice (from 1 to 2 lemons)
1 garlic clove
2 (15.5-ounce) cans chickpeas
2 teaspoons kosher salt
½ teaspoon baking soda
½ teaspoon ground cumin
½ cup tahini
2 ice cubes (the secret to extra-fluffy hummus)
Excellent quality olive oil and one of the Toppings (see chart, page 32, for garnish
Store-bought pita, Fluffy Pitas (page 134), or crudités, for serving

Pour the lemon juice into a small bowl. Grate the garlic clove directly in the bowl and set aside.

Pour the chickpeas into a colander. Rinse the chickpeas with cold water while shaking the colander until the cloudy foamy water washes off and the water is totally clear. (If your sink has a hose, now is the perfect time to use it.) Shake the colander again to drain, then pour the chickpeas into a large saucepan. Add 1 teaspoon of the salt, the baking soda, cumin, and 4 cups water.

Set over high heat until boiling, then reduce to medium-low and set a timer for 20 minutes. No need to stir or cover, just let them simmer away. When the timer goes off, carefully scoop out 2 tablespoons of the chickpea water and set that aside. Pour the chickpeas back into the colander to drain and let them sit for about 10 minutes until they're cool enough to handle.

This is where it gets a smidge tedious, but just for a moment! It's worth it if you want to put in the effort, but the world will not stop turning if you skip it. Scoop up a handful of chickpeas. Pinch off the skin of each one. Skins go in the trash; naked chickpea in a food processor. (If some skins end up in the processor, totally fine. Don't sacrifice a finger for the cause.) Hold a small mesh strainer over the food processor and pour the lemon juice through, discarding the garlic. Add that reserved chickpea water along with the tahini, ice cubes, and remaining 1 teaspoon salt.

Puree the mixture for 2 minutes until it's broken down into a gorgeously thick mixture. Use a rubber spatula to scrape down the sides and taste for seasoning. Then process for 2 more minutes, until it's unbelievably silky smooth.

*Recipe continues*

Lay out a piece of parchment and set your serving bowl upside down on it. Trace around the edge and cut out the parchment round—inside the line to avoid the ink. Turn the bowl right side up, then use a rubber spatula to scrape the hummus into the serving bowl and smooth the top. Press the parchment round onto the hummus and all around the edge. Without any preservatives, the hummus will naturally form a skin on top. This extra step is saving the world from that nightmare.

Hummus is meant to be served fresh so make this as close to go time as possible and keep it at room temperature. If you need to make it ahead, do the parchment, then cover the top of the bowl with plastic wrap and refrigerate for up to 24 hours. Set out at room temperature, still wrapped up, for at least 1 hour before serving.

Make the topping that speaks to you and pack that in a separate container. When it's time to serve, remove the parchment. Press a soup spoon in the center of the hummus and use your other hand to rotate the bowl to create a shallow crater in the center. Sprinkle or spoon the topping, or anything else from your imagination, in the crater then finish with a drizzle of really, really, really good olive oil. Serve with plenty of pita for ripping and dipping.

| TOPPINGS | |
| --- | --- |
| **CRUNCHY** | Roughly chop 2 tablespoons roasted, salted pistachios. Add to a small airtight container with 1 tablespoon toasted sesame seeds and ½ teaspoon ground cumin. Give it a good shake to mix. If you want, crush up 2 tablespoons French's Crispy Fried Onions and add to the mix. |
| **SPICY** | Drain a 4-ounce jar of pimento peppers and finely chop. Add to a small airtight container with 1 tablespoon spicy harissa and 1 teaspoon lemon juice. Give it a good stir to mix. If you want, stir in 1 tablespoon Greek yogurt or labneh for a creamy mix. |
| **HERBY** | In a small airtight container, combine 1 teaspoon dried mint, 1 teaspoon dried oregano, and 1 teaspoon dried parsley. Give it a good shake to mix. If you want, finely mince 2 tablespoons pitted, marinated olives and add to the mix. |

# White Beans + Tinned Fish

IN YOUR SLEEP | GF, NF

A can opener, a knife, and a fork are all it takes to make this dip. But even things that are entry-level effort have the right to feel impressive and considered. A quick soak of shallot and lemon juice gives a mellow onion experience, without that sharp pungency. Mashed cannellini and sour cream deliver pure fatty richness. Smoked fish and smoked paprika give it a—how can I put this?—smoky flavor. And fresh parsley (more helpful as a color than a flavor, in my opinion) makes it feel very finished. It's a total breeze and a total bull's-eye all in one bowl.

*(Pictured on page 79)*

**Makes 2 cups, enough for 6 people**

1 medium shallot
1 tablespoon fresh lemon juice
1 (15.5-ounce) can cannellini beans, drained and rinsed
¼ cup sour cream
1 (3.5-ounce) can smoked trout or any smoked fish
1 teaspoon kosher salt (see Party Tricks)
½ teaspoon freshly ground black pepper
½ teaspoon smoked paprika
2 tablespoons roughly chopped fresh parsley
Your favorite crackers or any store-bought or homemade carbs, like Fluffy Pitas (page 134), Cornmeal Crackers (page 123), or Seeded Barbari (page 137), for serving

Chop the shallot into small pieces, then run your knife back and forth to get as fine a mince as you can. Scoop the shallot into a medium bowl, then pour the lemon juice over top. Use a fork to mix—the acid in the lemon will help the shallot chill out—then let it sit for 2 minutes.

Add the beans to the same bowl and use the fork to mash them into rough pieces. Every bean should be broken, but not every bean needs to be smashed; a little texture is really nice. Add the sour cream and fish (if it's packed in oil, add that too; if it's packed in water, tilt the can to drain it as much as possible, but honestly don't stress about it). Mix with the fork to break up the fish in small chunks. Add the salt, pepper, paprika, and parsley and mix one more time until the seasonings are incorporated.

Transfer to a serving bowl and wrap tightly with plastic. Refrigerate until you're ready to go, or up to 2 days ahead of time. Serve with the carb of your choice.

## PARTY TRICKS

- A couple pinches of everything bagel seasoning is never a bad idea, especially here, instead of the salt.

- For a smoother, kind of taramasalata feeling, put everything except the parsley into a food processor and whiz until smooth. Fold in the parsley, then scrape into a serving bowl.

# Salt + Vinegar Salsa Verde

IN YOUR SLEEP | V, GF, NF

**Let me just get out in front of this before it becomes a scandal: This is not a salt-and-vinegar-flavored salsa, although that sounds incredible. This is a very easy and classic blend of the usual suspects—tomatillo, lime, onion, and cilantro, plus one special ingredient to make sure the salsa is as verde as possible. But back to the recipe title: It's because I refuse to eat it with anything other than salt-and-vinegar chips. I know, tortilla chips are already perfect with salsa, and you're right to say that. Just trust me—a salt-and-vin chip is an even more perfect partner for the natural acidity of the tomatillos. They really make this salsa sparkle with a huge pop of flavor!**

**Makes 3½ cups, enough for 10 people**

1 pound tomatillos
2 medium limes
1 medium white onion, quartered
1 cup packed fresh cilantro leaves and stems
1 jalapeño, whole or seeded (see Party Tricks)
4 garlic cloves
2 teaspoons kosher salt (see Party Tricks)
½ teaspoon ground coriander (optional)
1 ice cube (see Party Tricks)
Salt-and-vinegar potato chips, for serving

Peel the papery skins off the tomatillos and rinse them well under cold water to remove the bitter, sticky residue. (It's okay if they're still a little sticky after rinsing.) Cut the tomatillos into quarters. Add half of them into a blender and blend on high for 30 seconds to break them up and get some liquid going. Add the rest of the tomatillos, but don't blend yet.

Roll the limes with your palm to release the juices. Cut them in half and squeeze them into the blender. Add the onion, cilantro, jalapeño, garlic, salt, coriander (if using), and ice cube. Blend on high for about 2 minutes, stopping at some point to scrape down the sides, until the salsa is a little chunky but mostly smooth.

Pour into a serving bowl and wrap tightly with plastic. Refrigerate until you're ready to go, or up to 1 day ahead of time. Serve—and I'm sorry, again, this is nonnegotiable—with salt-and-vinegar chips.

## PARTY TRICKS

- If you're wild for mild, here's the easiest way to get rid of jalapeño seeds: Lay the entire jalapeño on a cutting board. Cut lengthwise to slice off the side, leaving the center intact. Use the stem to rotate so the cut side is down and cut the next side. Rotate, cut, rotate, cut. In the end you should have 4 ovals and a stem with seeds that you can discard.

- For can't-stop salsa, here's my secret: 1 teaspoon kosher salt and ½ teaspoon MSG. (It's okay, it's not the '90s anymore, we can use it!)

- Whenever you need a blended sauce to stay vibrant, drop in an ice cube! The ice crystals shock the cilantro and keep this salsa looking bright and fresh.

# Muhammara

IN YOUR SLEEP | V, GF

My friend Edy Massih is the dip daddy of Brooklyn, which makes sense because he's from Lebanon, a cultural center of great dips. He brought muhammara (that's *mah-HAH-mah-rah*) into my life a few years ago, and it's had a death grip on me ever since. My obsession has to do with how easy it is to make—walnuts, red peppers, and a couple pals in a food processor—essentially a few small gestures that add up to big flavor. When you're working your way through this chapter to become the dip daddy (gender neutral) of _____ [insert city but not Brooklyn unless you're Edy], I'm not going to be shocked if this becomes your favorite.

**Makes 2 cups, enough for 8 people**

1 garlic clove
1 tablespoon fresh lemon juice
1 cup walnuts
½ cup panko breadcrumbs
1 (16-ounce) jar or 2 (7-ounce) jars roasted red peppers, whatever's at your grocery
2 tablespoons pomegranate molasses (see Party Tricks)
1 teaspoon kosher salt
1 teaspoon Aleppo pepper (see Party Tricks)
1 teaspoon ground cumin
2 tablespoons extra-virgin olive oil
Chopped fresh parsley and pomegranate seeds (optional), for garnish
Store-bought pita or Fluffy Pitas (page 134), for serving

Grate the garlic clove directly into a small bowl, then add the lemon juice. Let that sit so the garlic mellows.

In a small skillet, arrange the walnuts in an even layer. Set over medium heat, tossing or stirring occasionally. Use your knuckles to carefully press on the tops of the walnuts; when they feel hot, usually 3 to 4 minutes, remove the skillet from the stove. Immediately pour in the panko and toss or stir for a minute or two to very lightly toast. (This is about getting the raw flavor out of the panko, so don't worry about getting them golden brown.) Scrape everything into a food processor.

Drain the peppers and add to the food processor, along with the pomegranate molasses, salt, Aleppo pepper, cumin, and lemon-garlic mixture. Process for about 1 minute, then stop and use a rubber spatula to scrape down the sides. Add the olive oil and process for another minute, until the walnuts and peppers are finely chopped but the dip has nice texture. Taste for seasoning. I've been known to add another ¼ teaspoon of salt here, but it's up to you.

Scrape into a shallow bowl. Lightly press the spatula in the center while using your other hand to rotate the bowl, creating an even circle of dip with a crater in the center. Cover the bowl tightly with plastic wrap and refrigerate until you're ready to go, or up to 2 days ahead of time. Just before serving, sprinkle fresh parsley over the top, a little drizzle of olive oil wouldn't hurt either, and some pomegranate seeds are gorgeous if you really feel like going for it. Serve with pita for tearing and dipping.

## PARTY TRICKS

- If you want to make this nut-free, swap in 1 cup of pumpkin seeds. Use your eyes, not your knuckles, when they're in the skillet: lightly brown and they're done.

- If pomegranate molasses is hard to track down, use 1 tablespoon balsamic vinegar with 1 tablespoon honey as an approximation.

- Muhammara comes from Aleppo, Syria, so the signature smoky pepper flakes of the city are a key part of this dip. If you can get your hands on a jar, you're in for a treat. If not, totally fine to leave them out.

# Pico de Sandia

ROLL UP YOUR SLEEVES | V, GF, NF

I prefer *sandia* ("watermelon" in Spanish) to *tomate* (I bet you can guess that one) in *pico de gallo* ("rooster's beak," don't ask me why). It looks pretty much the same when everything is chopped up, but the sturdier texture and sweeter flavor bring a pleasing something extra to the bowl. I like a quick little pre-drain—it's going to be juicy no matter what, and really that's the joy of a good pico—to pull out some water and concentrate the flavors before mixing and letting the salsa macerate to perfection.

**Makes 7 cups, enough for 10 people**

1 (3½-pound) watermelon wedge, or 2½ pounds chopped watermelon
2 tablespoons granulated sugar
1 large red onion
3 medium limes
2 bell peppers, maybe yellow or orange for contrast
3 tablespoons Tajín (see Party Trick)
Very sturdy tortilla chips, for serving

## PARTY TRICK

- If you're having trouble finding Tajín, try 2 tablespoons chili powder or 2 tablespoons ground sumac mixed with 1 tablespoon kosher salt.

If your watermelon has a rind, use a vegetable peeler to remove only the green. The white part of the rind has a mild cucumber-ish flavor and a nice crunch, we can work with that! Set a cutting board inside a rimmed baking sheet to catch all the good juices that are about to flow.

Cut the watermelon into ¼-inch-thick pieces. Stack a few of the pieces and cut into ¼-inch-thick strips. Rotate the baking sheet a quarter turn and cut across to make ¼-inch cubes. Take a moment to discard any seeds as you work. Scoop the cubes (including the whites!) into a big bowl. Keep working your way through the watermelon—you'll end up with about 6 cups of cubes.

Tilt the baking sheet over the bowl to pour out the collected juices. Sprinkle the sugar over the watermelon and use a rubber spatula to mix it in. Cover the bowl with a clean kitchen towel, move it out of the way, and set a timer for 30 minutes. Give your cutting board a quick wash and dry, then dice the onion, aiming for the same size as the watermelon. Move the diced onion to a small bowl and fill it with cold water. Put it in the refrigerator and let it soak while the watermelon rests.

When the timer goes off, set a mesh strainer or colander with small holes over a medium bowl—for your mental health, please do this in the sink. Pour the watermelon and juice into the strainer, give it a few good shakes, and tip the watermelon back into the bowl it just came from. (That delicious bowl of watermelon juice is all yours, baby!) Pour the onions into the same strainer, give them a rinse under cold water, and a shake to drain, then add to the bowl with the watermelon.

Roll the limes with your palm to release the juices. Cut in half and squeeze those into the bowl. Dice the bell pepper, aiming for the same size as the watermelon, and add to the bowl along with the Tajín. Mix everything together, then cover the bowl tightly with plastic wrap. Refrigerate for at least 1 hour before serving or up to 2 days. The salsa will slowly submerge itself in delicious juices, so make sure to serve with strong tortilla chips that can handle it.

# Vegan Elote Queso

ROLL UP YOUR SLEEVES | V, GF, NF

Corn kernels are—get this!—packed with cornstarch. It seems so obvious typing it now, but I'm not afraid to say that revelation took me a couple days to process. Like the pâté on page 27, this is vegan witchcraft. Liquifying the corn and heating it slowly makes a thick, creamy "queso" that is simply corn, water, and nothing else. And since we're working with Big Corn Energy anyway, it only seemed natural to layer on classic elote flavors and finish the job: lime juice, cilantro, chili powder, and nutritional yeast for a cheesy touch. Even if you don't identify as vegan, you're going to be obsessed with this dip.

**Makes 3 cups, enough for 8 people**

4 cups corn kernels (see Party Tricks)
2 medium limes
¼ cup chopped fresh cilantro leaves and stems
⅓ cup nutritional yeast
1½ tablespoons kosher salt
1 teaspoon smoked paprika
1 teaspoon chili powder mix
Tortilla chips, for serving

In a blender, combine the corn with 2 cups boiling water. Set a timer for 5 minutes so the kernels can soften, then blend on low for about 2 minutes, until the corn is completely broken down. Set a medium mesh strainer over a large liquid cup measure and pour the mixture through, stopping occasionally to use a rubber spatula to stir—not press!—the pulp to let the liquid through. You should end up with 3 to 3½ cups of corn juice. Top off the measuring cup with water to hit an even 4 cups.

Put an apron on, this can get messy. Pour the liquid into a medium saucepan and set over low heat. Set a timer for 15 minutes. Use the rubber spatula to stir the liquid constantly, focusing on keeping the bottom moving and scraping down the sides so nothing scorches. When the timer goes off, it should be just starting to thicken—you know when you microwave a jar of queso and it's super liquidy but also kind of gloopy? That texture. Remove the saucepan from the stove and set a timer for 30 minutes. It'll continue to thicken as it sits.

When the timer goes off, roll the limes under your palm to release the juices. Cut them in half and squeeze them into the saucepan, along with the cilantro, nutritional yeast, salt, paprika, and chili powder. Whisk until everything is completely combined. Taste for seasoning—remember, tortilla chips are salty, so trying a bite in context is a great idea—then use the rubber spatula to scrape into a serving bowl. Press plastic wrap directly onto the surface and hold at room temperature until it's time to serve (see Party Tricks). Give it a little stir just before serving and set out plenty of tortilla chips for dipping.

## PARTY TRICKS

- The corn can come from three 15.25-ounce cans that have been drained, 6 large cobs, or one 16-ounce bag of frozen corn. Just between us, I found that the frozen corn actually has the best flavor and—bonus!—it's also the easiest because it can go straight from the freezer into the blender.

- It's best if you can make this on the day you're serving it and keep at room temperature, but if you need to make it ahead, press plastic on the surface and refrigerate for up to 48 hours. Before serving, remove the plastic, add ¼ cup water and microwave in 30-second bursts, stopping to stir between each one, until it's a little warm but a bit loose.

# Whipped Blue Cheese

IN YOUR SLEEP | VG, GF, NF

Eating crudités is a metaphysical act of balancing as much dip as possible on a thin strip of carrot, then laughing in the face of gravity and good manners as you race towards your tongue. This whipped mix of sweet gorgonzola (or whatever blue cheese you're into), goat cheese, tarragon, and dill is on the thick side for easy dipping, but it's also on the delicious side so you absolutely will not be behaving yourself. Speaking of *being bad*, you can also blow things up by adding a second bowl of dip to the veggie platter. (Please see Herb Salad with Homemade Ranch on page 74, and you already know exactly which part of that recipe I'm talking about.)

**Makes 1½ cups, enough for 6 people**

4 ounces Gorgonzola Dolce or any blue cheese
4 ounces goat cheese
½ cup heavy cream
Juice of 1 lemon
2 tablespoons roughly chopped tarragon, plus a little more for garnish
2 tablespoons roughly chopped dill, plus a little more for garnish
Freshly ground black pepper
Extra-virgin olive oil, for drizzling
Crudités, such as green beans, carrots sticks, chopped celery, separated endive, cucumber spears, sliced bell peppers, halved radishes, and broccoli florets, for serving

In a medium bowl, combine the Gorgonzola, goat cheese, lemon juice, cream, tarragon, dill, and a bunch of good cracks of pepper. Use a fork to mash the cheeses, then switch to a handheld mixer to whip until the mixture is nice and fluffy, about 2 minutes. (Or use a regular whisk and a lot of elbow grease.) Taste for seasoning—depending on how strong your blue cheese was you might feel like adding a pinch of salt here. Use a rubber spatula to scrape into a small serving bowl. It can be served right away or wrapped with plastic wrap, refrigerated for up to 3 days, and brought to room temperature 30 minutes ahead of time.

To serve, use a spoon to swirl the cheese in cute little peaks and valleys, then drizzle some olive oil on top and add a nice sprinkle of herbs and a couple more cracks of pepper. Don't forget to make a lovely little nest of crudités around your dip.

# RAISE
# THE BAR

**TRUST ME,** I am not above a melting bucket of seltzer and beer, or a sticky counter of alcohol and mixers. But if everyone shows up with a cheap bottle of bubbly, it literally becomes a Champagne problem. Wouldn't it be nice if someone brought a little vision to the drinks? You are now that someone, with a range of nonalcoholic, alcohol-optional, and boozy punches, drinks, and shots. In a room full of cans and bottles, I dare you to be the *signature cocktail*.

# Spiced Hibiscus Punch

IN YOUR SLEEP | V, GF, NF, NA

We're all grown-ups here, so there is no excuse for a boring bowl of punch. Even without alcohol, this is as far from a school dance as it can possibly be. Hibiscus flowers (you might be familiar with their work in agua de jamaica or Red Zinger tea bags) have a kind of cranberry tartness that pairs really well with mulling spices and citrus. Find the spiciest ginger beer (not ginger ale, we're leaving the past behind) you can for a bubbly, burning background to your fruity party drink. Balancing a floating ring of decorative ice in the bowl is the perfect cinematic final touch.

*(Pictured on page 63)*

**Makes 11 cups, enough for 15 people**

1 cup dried hibiscus flowers (see Party Tricks)
1 cup sugar
4 thyme sprigs
2 cinnamon sticks
6 star anise pods
¾ cup fresh grapefruit juice (from 1 grapefruit)
¼ cup fresh lime juice (from 2 to 3 limes)
4 (12-ounce) bottles extra-strong ginger beer of your choice
1 (12-ounce) can seltzer
Ice ring (see Party Tricks), for serving

### SPECIAL EQUIPMENT
3-quart punch bowl and decorative ladle
Plastic tumblers or punch cups

In a large saucepan, combine the hibiscus, sugar, thyme, cinnamon, star anise, and 3 cups water. Bring to a boil over high heat, then reduce to the lowest possible heat, cover, and set a timer for 30 minutes. When the timer goes off, remove from the heat and strain the liquid into a large punch bowl. Cool completely, about 1 hour.

Add the grapefruit juice and lime juice to the bowl and just before serving, pour in the ginger beer and seltzer. Add the ice ring, drop in the ladle, set out the cups, and let everyone serve themselves.

## PARTY TRICKS

- Hibiscus flowers can be found online or in a Mexican grocery. Hibiscus tea bags will also work in a pinch; use 8 so the tea is strong.

- If you're making this to go, strain the hibiscus tea into an airtight container and refrigerate for up to 3 days. Add the grapefruit and lime juices to the container just before leaving, and pack the bowl, ice ring, ginger beer, and seltzer to assemble on arrival.

- To make an ice ring, simply grab a Bundt pan, tube pan, or cake pan that is smaller than your punch bowl, spread a layer of fruit, then lay some sprigs of fresh herbs on top. For a wintery touch, I like to use pomegranate seeds and rosemary. For a summery feeling, I like thinly sliced limes and mint. Let your imagination be your guide. Slowly pour in 2 cups cold water and freeze overnight. To unmold, hold the pan upside down in your hands and run the bottom under warm tap water until the ice ring falls in your hands. Float the prettiest side in the punch bowl.

# Whole Lemon Lemonade

IN YOUR SLEEP | V, GF, NF, NA

A lemonade made from the whole lemon is the only life I've ever known. Peel, pith, seeds, and fruit get mashed together for the most intensely all-caps **LEMON** lemonade you've ever had—all tart, zero bitter. I love a little splash of rose water for a perfect floral accent—orange blossom water and mint extract accomplish a similarly gorgeous vibe—but it's truly perfect on its own, too. When life gives you lemons, throw them in the blender and let 'er rip!

**Makes 4 cups, enough for 8 people**

4 large lemons
¾ cup granulated sugar (or 1 cup if you like it extra sweet)
½ teaspoon kosher salt
1 tablespoon rose water or orange blossom water or 2 teaspoons mint extract (optional)
Ice
Edible rose petals or a sprinkle of ground sumac (optional)

Quarter each lemon, then slice into roughly ¼-inch pieces. Transfer the lemon pieces to a medium bowl and sprinkle the sugar and salt on top. Set a timer for 15 minutes to let the lemons soften. When the timer goes off, use a potato masher, a cocktail muddler, or a big wooden spoon to aggressively smash the lemon pieces, breaking down the fruit and rinds into a pool of juice.

Stir in 3 cups of very cold water until it feels like the sugar is dissolved. Set a fine-mesh strainer over a quart container. (Save the tears and do this in the sink.) Slowly pour the lemonade through the strainer, then squeeze the lemon carcasses to get the last of that good flavor. Add the rose water or any flavoring, if that's what you want, then slowly pour in cold water as needed to hit the full quart. Cover and refrigerate for at least 1 hour or up to 3 days. Shake well before serving.

To serve, pack an 8-ounce cup with ice and then fill with lemonade (about ½ cup). If you're really looking to make an impression, crush and sprinkle some rose petals on top, or a pinch of vibrant sumac, or both!

## PARTY TRICKS

- If pink lemonade is what your heart really wants, add 2 sliced strawberries to the smash pile.

- If a shot of vodka finds its way into the glasses (of the willing!!!), that's a-okay with me.

Arnie Palmer,
50

Whole Lemon
Lemonade

# Arnie Palmer

ROLL UP YOUR SLEEVES | V, GF, NF, NA

At his dead-end middle-management job, he's Arnold. But as soon as he hits the white sands and crystal-clear waters in his Tommy Bahama shirt, well that's Arnie. This twist on a classic—green tea! limeade! coconut milk!—is our guy loosening his tie and living a little. I'm partial to the vegetal umami of a good green tea here, but I made you a little chart if you want to dip a toe into, say, oolong or mint or Earl Grey, or even a blend of a couple different teas. (And yes, *Arnold*, there is a note for black tea here and a recipe for lemonade on page 48.)

**Makes enough for 8 people**

Ice
4 cups Iced Tea (recipe follows)
4 cups Limeade (recipe follows)

SPECIAL EQUIPMENT
Cocktail umbrellas and
   maraschino cherries, if the
   budget allows

Pack a 16-ounce cup to the top with ice. Fill halfway (about ½ cup) with the iced tea, then top off (another ½ cup) with the limeade. Drop in a straw before serving. It's very cute to diagonally stab a cocktail umbrella through a maraschino cherry and let them both lounge on the edge of the cup.

## PARTY TRICKS

- This method works with any variety of tea. Ideal steeping temps are 170°F to 185°F for green or white, 180°F to 190°F for oolong, and 205°F to 210°F for black or herbal.

- If you're serious about your tea, you probably already have a method for making sure the water is exactly the right temperature. For the rest of us, here are visual cues to get close enough: 180°F is a few tiny bubbles around the perimeter rapidly breaking, 190°F is slightly larger bubbles around the edge and the center is jiggling like an earthquake, and 210°F is when it's a second away from breaking out into a full boil.

# Iced Tea

**Makes 4 cups**

6 green tea bags, or any type
   you love, paper tags removed
2 cups ice

In a small saucepan, bring 2 cups water up to temp (see Party Tricks). Remove from the heat and add the tea bags. Swirl to submerge the tea bags, then cover and steep for 5 minutes. Swirl again, then discard the tea bags. Pour the tea into the quart container and immediately add the ice. Cover and refrigerate for at least 1 hour or up to 1 week.

# Limeade

**Makes 4 cups**

8 medium limes
¾ cup granulated sugar (or
   1 cup if you like it extra sweet)
½ teaspoon kosher salt
1 cup boiling water
1 (13.5-ounce) can full-fat
   coconut milk (shake it hard
   before opening)

Zest 4 of the limes into a medium bowl. Add the sugar and salt, then get in there with your fingers and pinch away until all that sugar is bright green and super fragrant. Pour the boiling water into the bowl, then slowly stir until the sugar is dissolved. Set a timer for 30 minutes to let the mixture cool.

Meanwhile, juice all 8 of the limes, or as many as it takes to hit ⅔ cup of juice. When the zesty mixture is cooled, stir in the lime juice and coconut milk. Set a fine-mesh strainer over a quart container, and I beg you once more to do this in the sink. Pour the liquid through, then lift the strainer to let the last of it drip past the zest. Top off with cold water as needed to hit the full quart. Cover and refrigerate for at least 1 hour or up to 3 days. Shake well before serving.

*Seasoned Oyster Crackers, 224*

# Surfer on Acid

IN YOUR SLEEP | V, GF

When I moved to New York as a teenager, I used to sneak into a dive bar in midtown and the bartender, Cindy, introduced me to Surfer on Acid as a shot. I kind of forgot about it for a couple decades until recently when I ended up with a bottle of Jäger (something I also kind of forgot about for a couple decades) and the memory came rushing back. If the thought of Jäger makes you want to vom, I get it, but I beg you to give it one more try. It's actually a complex digestif that should be held up alongside Fernet and Averna, but has suffered decades of bad PR. Mixed with pineapple and lime, it's a little tiki, a little bitter, perfectly sippable, and very delicious.

**Makes 1 drink**

1 ounce Jägermeister
1 ounce pineapple rum
1 ounce canned pineapple juice
½ ounce orgeat (see Party Tricks)
½ ounce fresh lime juice (from ½ lime)
Ice

Measure and combine the Jäger, rum, pineapple juice, orgeat, and lime juice in a shaker filled with ice. Shake, shake, shake, really go for it, until the outside of the shaker is frosty like a winter window and your hand is chilly. Strain into a rocks glass with ice and slide that baby across the bar with a wink (jk, please do not ever do that). But please do swap out the shaker ice before making the next drink.

To batch the drink, mix 1 cup each of Jäger, rum, and pineapple juice with ½ cup each of orgeat and lime juice in a quart jar. (This will make 8 drinks or 16 shots total.) When it's time to serve, give the jar a quick shake to mix. Measure out ½ cup (or 4 ounces) of the mixture into a shaker, shake, and serve on the rocks or as shots. Give the jar a little shake before making each drink and—say it with me—swap out the shaker ice.

## PARTY TRICKS

- Orgeat—pronounced *or-ZJAT* (I bombed that at a liquor store once and it was awful)—is just a chic almond syrup. The bitters brand Fee Brothers makes a cutie little bottle and Torani makes a big pump bottle. If you can't find it (or just don't feel like looking), mix ½ cup agave with 1 tablespoon pure almond extract. That will get you through 8 drinks.

- To make shots, follow the cocktail directions but strain into two shot glasses. Remember to swap out the shaker ice before making the next round of shots.

# Picklebacks

Yes, technically this is a recipe for pickles with a bottle of whiskey tacked on at the end, but let me explain. There are few things as joyful and pure in this world as the second lease on life you get from a pickleback. For the uninitiated, you hold a shot of whiskey in one hand and a shot of pickle juice in the other. You down the whiskey, and shiver on cue, but then immediately follow up with the pickle juice and it wipes the slate clean, you're a newborn baby who has never known troubles or strife. When I was in my twenties, I showed up to every birthday party with a batch of homemade pickles and a bottle of Four Roses. My friends have mostly aged out of shots now, but I still pull this trick on special occasions. It's a move that will never let you down, no matter what age you are.

**Makes enough brine for 12 shots or 1 really good quart of pickles**

6 big dill sprigs
1 teaspoon whole black peppercorns
1 teaspoon coriander seeds
3 garlic cloves
4 Persian or mini cucumbers (see Party Tricks)
2 tablespoons sugar
1 tablespoon kosher salt
1 cup vinegar (see Party Tricks)
¼ teaspoon calcium chloride (see Party Tricks; optional)
1 (750-ml) bottle whiskey or bourbon

On a cutting board, make a little dill nest with the peppercorns and coriander seeds safely in the center. Roll a 1-quart jar over everything to lightly crush the dill and kind of crack some spices. Don't go nuts, this is just to wake up extra flavor. The dill and spices go into the jar.

Next, use the flat side of a knife to smash the garlic cloves. You can pick the skins off or leave them on, it doesn't matter. (I leave them on because I believe in my heart they add flavor.) Toss them into the jar.

Line up your cucumbers and trim off the nubs on both ends. (One nub has an enzyme that makes pickles mushy and I can never remember which, so I trim both to be safe.) Slice into ¼-inch-thick rounds and—you guessed it!—straight into the jar.

Also in the jar: the sugar, salt, vinegar, 1 cup of cold water, and the calcium chloride, if you're feeling especially type A. It's important to pour in the vinegar before the water because your jar might run out of room for liquid; we want to prioritize the good stuff. If the opposite happens and your jar still has some extra room, top it off with more vinegar.

Screw the lid on tight and shake until the salt and sugar are dissolved and maybe shake a little more just to be sure. The jar goes in the fridge for at least 24 hours, ideally 1 week for great flavor, and up to 1 month if you're really planning ahead.

To serve, pour a shot of whiskey in one glass and a shot of pickle juice in the other glass. Shoot the whiskey first and then immediately shoot the pickle juice.

## PARTY TRICKS

- Any type of cuke will work, but Persian (sometimes they go by "mini") are the crispiest, in my experience.

- Let's talk about that vinegar. Use at least ½ cup of distilled white vinegar, because it's cheap and does the job. For that other ½ cup, keep pouring the distilled or, for a little more oomph, grab any light-colored vin like Champagne, rice (unseasoned!), white balsamic, or white wine.

- You can sometimes find calcium chloride if your grocery has a section for serious canners, but it's definitely orderable online. It keeps the pickles extra crunchy, but it's not going to make or break the brine.

- Switch out the seasonings: Any color peppercorns are great as are cumin seeds, dried chiles, dried seaweed, everything bagel seasoning, fennel seeds, grains of paradise, mustard seeds, nigella seeds, Old Bay, sesame seeds, togarashi, za'atar, whatever tickles your pickle.

*Aperol Spritz*

*Dirty Shirley*

*Piña Colada*

# Jell-O Cocktail Shots

ROLL UP YOUR SLEEVES | GF, NF

You can put lipstick on a pig, but it's still a Jell-O shot. Is that how it goes? Anyway, the point is these are Jell-O shots through and through, but instead of questioning if your shot could also take off your nail polish, a simple investment in good alcohol with a key mixer makes it all so much more enjoyable. Three Jell-O flavors act as the base for three of my favorite easy cocktails: Dirty Shirley, Aperol Spritz, and Piña Colada. Make one, make all three, just make enough because these will go quick!

## Each flavor makes 12 shots

½ cup boiling water
1 (3-ounce) box flavored Jell-O
1 cup mixer
½ cup alcohol
1 envelope unflavored Jell-O

### SPECIAL EQUIPMENT
Plastic shot glasses with lids

In a small bowl, measure and pour the boiling water, then whisk in the Jell-O until dissolved. In a 4-cup liquid measuring cup, measure the mixer and alcohol together, then sprinkle the unflavored gelatin over top. Let the gelatin bloom for about 5 minutes, until it looks thick and clumpy. Pour the warm Jell-O mixture into the measuring cup and slowly whisk until all the gelatin is dissolved. (Whisking too fast will make the mixture overly foamy.)

Line up 12 shot cups with lids. Measure and pour 1½ ounces into each cup and snap the lid on top. There might be a little leftover liquid, which is your little reward/taste test. Stack the cups and chill in the refrigerator for at least 4 hours, until fully set, or up to 3 days in advance.

| | DIRTY SHIRLEY | APEROL SPRITZ | PIÑA COLADA |
|---|---|---|---|
| **FLAVORED JELL-O** | 1 (3-ounce) box cherry Jell-O | 1 (3-ounce) box orange Jell-O | 1 (3-ounce) box pineapple Jell-O |
| **MIXER** | 1 cup Sprite | 1 cup prosecco | 1 cup cream of coconut* |
| **ALCOHOL** | ½ cup vodka | ½ cup Aperol | ½ cup coconut rum |

* Make sure to buy the sweetened cream of coconut (Coco López, for example), not coconut cream or coconut milk which also come in cans and are probably stacked on the same shelf.

# Pitcher-Perfect Margaritas

IN YOUR SLEEP | V, GF, NF

I'm sorry if this is controversial, but I do not care for rims on drinks—salt, sugar, or otherwise. I've never totally mastered the rhythm of lick-sip, so it mostly becomes a barrier between me and my alcohol until I clear a path wide enough for normal drinking. When it comes to mixing a margarita, I prefer to put salt inside the drink instead, which still gives it a little oomph with a much better user experience. (Smoked salt is even smarter, for a mezcal suggestion at a tequila price.) This recipe is scaled up to pitcher size and, let's not pussyfoot around here, you should probably double it.

**Makes 4 cups, enough for 8 people**

2 cups blanco tequila
1 cup fresh lime juice (from 8 to 10 limes)
½ cup Pierre Ferrand Dry Curaçao or Grand Marnier
½ cup agave
1 teaspoon smoked salt or flaky sea salt (optional)
Ice

In a pitcher that can hold at least 4½ cups (36 ounces), stir together the tequila, lime juice, curaçao, agave, and salt, if you're adding it. Then, stay with me here, stir in ¼ cup of cold water. The water slightly dilutes the drink, mimicking what would naturally be happening in a cocktail shaker, and water weirdly helps open everything up and taste more like a margarita and less like a tequila assault. Cover the pitcher with plastic wrap and keep chilled until it's party time, but no more than 8 hours. Give it a good stir before serving. Pack an 8-ounce cup with ice, pour in ½ cup of margarita, and serve.

If you're home alone and feeling like a cheeky marg, combine 2 ounces tequila, 1 ounce lime juice, ½ ounce curaçao, and ½ ounce agave in a shaker filled with ice. (Perhaps a pinch of salt?) Shake like you mean it until the outside of the shaker looks like the car window in *Titanic*. Strain into a rocks glass with ice.

## PARTY TRICK

- For extra credit, zest the limes before juicing, soak the zest in the fresh juice for 15 minutes, then strain the juice and discard the zest. (Set that timer because any longer than 15 and the zest will start to get bitter.)

# Staycation

IN YOUR SLEEP | V, GF, NF

When you wish you were sipping a spritz in Europe but your PTO didn't get approved, this backyard version will mellow your sorrows. St-Germain, a sweet elderflower liqueur, and Suze, a bitter, citrusy liqueur—two French aperitifs, almost like you're there!!—mingle with Modelo beer for a lightly boozy, effervescent drink that will make you sparkle from the inside out. And to those of you new to drinking beer over ice, welcome to the club, you're going to love it here! Spritzes really need to be made to order; batching is not ideal. But as you get the hang of it, you can probably stop measuring and just eyeball. By your second spritz, I promise every pour is going to feel perfect and exactly right.

**Makes 1 drink**

Ice
2 ounces St-Germain
1 ounce Suze
6 ounces Modelo Especial or
  any Mexican lager
Juice of ½ lime
Orange slices, for serving

Fill a wineglass halfway with ice. Measure and pour the Lillet and Suze and stir a couple times to mix. Top with the Modelo (6 ounces is half a can or bottle, if you want to just eyeball it) and squeeze in the lime half. Stir twice to mix. Slip an orange slice into the glass, slide in a straw, and serve.

## PARTY TRICKS

- Slice all your fruit at home and pack in an airtight container. It's a nice little touch to be a nice little guest.

- Check if your host has wine glasses or bring 12-ounce clear plastic cups. Bring straws no matter what.

# Hazelnut Eggnog

BRAGGING RIGHTS | VG, GF (NF)

Let's talk about one of my favorite holiday drinks: eggnog. I wait all year for that post-Halloween period when grocery stores push the coffee creamers aside and start stocking eggnog—and how much of it I drink in Q4 is really none of your business. But when it's party time, homemade is the only answer because the difference between a bowl of *real* eggnog and anything you could get in the carton is night and day. This is one smooth puppy: not too sweet, slightly eggy, egregiously boozy, and topped with an Arctic Sea of floating egg-white-and-whipped-cream icebergs. It's a stunning visual feast and a drink that goes down a little too easy.

## Makes 14 cups, enough for 18 people

¼ cup hazelnuts, plus a few more for garnish
1 quart whole milk
12 large eggs
2 cups granulated sugar
1 quart plus 1 pint heavy cream, very cold
1½ cups bourbon (or a 375 ml bottle)
1½ cups spiced rum (or a 375 ml bottle)

### SPECIAL EQUIPMENT
8-quart (or 2-gallon) punch bowl and decorative ladle

In a small skillet, spread the hazelnuts in an even layer. Set over medium heat and toast, tossing occasionally, until warm and fragrant, about 10 minutes. Pour the hazelnuts onto a clean kitchen towel. Gather the sides of the towel up and rub it all around between your hands to get the skins off. Pick out the hazelnuts and drop them into a blender (a few stray skins are totally fine). Pour about half of the milk into the blender—just eyeball it, it doesn't need to be exact—and blend on high for about 2 minutes until the hazelnuts are pulverized.

Set out an 8-quart (or 2-gallon) punch bowl and a large airtight container next to each other. Crack the eggs, one at a time, dropping the whites into the airtight container and the yolks into the punch bowl. Cover and refrigerate the whites. Add the sugar to the yolk bowl and whisk with all your elbow grease until the yolks are thick and pale yellow, about 5 minutes.

Add the hazelnut mixture to the bowl. Pour the rest of the milk into the blender and swirl it around to get any last bits, then pour that into the bowl, too. Crack open the quart of cream and tip that in as well. Whisk away until everything is completely mixed, then add the bourbon and rum and whisk once more. Cover the bowl tightly with plastic wrap and refrigerate for at least 2 hours, or up to 2 days ahead.

Before serving, uncover the punch bowl, put the ladle in, and give it a good stir to bring the nog back to life. Pour the egg whites into a large bowl and use a handheld mixer to beat on medium speed until stiff peaks form, about 6 minutes. Tip the whites into the punch bowl. Pour the pint of cold cream into the same bowl and beat on medium until stiff peaks form, about 3 minutes. Scoop the whipped cream into the bowl. Use the ladle to stir, letting some of the whites and cream mix in but leaving most casually floating on top.

As a final touch, use a rasp to grate a few hazelnuts (with the skin on) over the punch bowl just before serving. Set out the cups and let everyone scoop their own eggnog.

## PARTY TRICKS

- I love the warm accent of hazelnuts, but if that's a step too far or you need to avoid nuts, this recipe is equally excellent without them.

- Arrange with your host ahead of time so you can come over early and make this before everyone gets there. (Do not surprise them with a huge bowl of eggnog!) This makes a ton of nog, so cut it in half if you're not trying to overload on holiday cheer.

# Amaro Hot Chocolate

IN YOUR SLEEP | VG, GF, NF (NA)

Amaro, an herbal, bittersweet digestif, is a surprisingly wonderful partner to a warm cup of hot chocolate, making it just a little more complex than usual. Baileys, a mixture of cream, cocoa, and whiskey, slips in unnoticed and makes it feel a little more rich. And even if you choose to make this without alcohol, mixing cocoa powder with dark brown sugar gives it an uncommon depth of flavor besides the usual chocolaty and sweet. The mini marshmallows are optional but very strongly recommended for an extra touch of holiday cheer.

**Makes 18 cups, enough for 18 people**

1 cup packed dark brown sugar
1 cup unsweetened Dutch-
  processed cocoa powder
1 cup amaro, preferably
  Averna
1 cup Baileys
1 gallon whole milk
Mini marshmallows (optional),
  for serving

In a Dutch oven, whisk the brown sugar and cocoa powder together until there are no lumps.

Set the Dutch oven on the stove and whisk in the booze until the sugar and cocoa are starting to dissolve. Pour in the milk and whisk until everything is completely combined. Set over low heat and cover. It should take about 45 minutes to warm up. Remove the lid and whisk one more time to make sure it's all combined. Drop the ladle in, set out cups and mini marshmallows, and let everyone go to town.

## PARTY TRICKS

- If you're making this to go, put the lid on the Dutch oven after whisking the sugar and cocoa. Combine the amaro and Baileys in an airtight container. The milk, marshmallows, and cups are already packed for you. Ask your host ahead of time if you can borrow a whisk and a ladle and hog a burner all night.

- This makes a huge batch of hot chocolate, but the recipe can easily be cut in half for a more polite serving.

CHANGE OF GREENERY

**WHEN YOU'RE INVITED** to a party that needs something more substantial, like a picnic, BBQ, or dinner party, let your host worry about the main character while you swoop in with a quirky supporting best friend. There are no wimpy, lifeless salads here, only big flavors and sturdy ingredients that can sit out all afternoon and still feel fresh.

# Caesar Salad with Bouillon Crouton

ROLL UP YOUR SLEEVES | VG, GF, NF

I love big croutons, but I hate feeling like my gums are under attack. And I love anchovies more than life itself, but I don't love an anchovy dressing sitting out in the sun all day. So we're going to solve for both problems in this salad. Croutons: Big chunks of torn bread get tossed in bouillon and *lightly* toasted so they're crunchy on the outside but pillowy inside. (Sidebar: I love making this with chicken bouillon for an incredible chicken Caesar feeling, but I've made it with vegetable bouillon, too, and honestly, no complaints.) Anchovies: We're ditching them entirely. This stealth Caesar dressing starts with hummus as a creamy base, meaning no pressure to nail an emulsification, then layers on a bunch of acidic, savory, briny ingredients to help you fly undetected.

**Serves 6 to 8**

### CAESAR DRESSING
½ cup hummus, store-bought or homemade (page 30)
Juice of 1 lemon
2 garlic cloves
¼ cup grated Parmesan cheese
2 tablespoons capers plus 2 teaspoons caper brine
2 tablespoons extra-virgin olive oil
2 tablespoons Dijon mustard
4 teaspoons soy sauce or tamari
2 ice cubes
2 teaspoons freshly ground black pepper
1 teaspoon kosher salt

### CROUTONS
1 (12- to 16-ounce) loaf soft Italian or French bread, gluten-free if you want
¼ cup extra-virgin olive oil
1 tablespoon vegetable or chicken bouillon paste, like Better Than Bouillon

**Make the dressing:** In a blender, combine—in this order—the hummus, lemon juice, garlic cloves, Parmesan, capers and brine, the olive oil and Dijon mustard (in alternating tablespoons so the mustard slides out), soy sauce, ice cubes, pepper, and salt. Blend on high until the ice cubes go silent and the dressing is completely smooth, about 1 minute. It's great now, but it's better later so pour it into an airtight container and refrigerate for up to 2 days. (This makes 1⅓ cups of dressing.)

**Make the croutons:** Preheat the oven to 450°F. Line a rimmed baking sheet with parchment paper.

Tear the bread into roughly 1-inch pieces with irregular edges. Arrange the croutons on the prepared baking sheet. In a small bowl, whisk the olive oil and bouillon together, then drizzle it over the croutons and toss to coat.

Slide the baking sheet into the oven and set a timer for 4 minutes. Flip the croutons over, then set a timer for 4 more minutes. At this point they should be a little crunchy on the surface but soft inside. Give them 2 more minutes if you think they need it, then set aside to cool on the baking sheet.

*Ingredients and recipe continue*

## SALAD

2 romaine hearts
4 ounces Parmesan cheese
Freshly ground black pepper
2 lemons, cut into wedges

**Make the salad:** Lay a romaine heart on a cutting board. Slice it lengthwise, starting at the top and stopping just before the root. Flip the heart a quarter turn and slice lengthwise again, stopping before the root. Now cut across in 1-inch pieces, stopping just before the root, for perfectly bite-size lettuce. Do it all over again with the other heart. Now do everyone a favor and wash that lettuce in cold water and dry it well.

In a large bowl, toss the romaine and ⅓ cup of the dressing until coated. Take a taste and decide if you need another tablespoon of dressing. Use a vegetable peeler to shave about half the Parmesan in long strips directly into the bowl, then switch to a rasp grater to grate the rest. Toss once or twice to make sure the cheese gets evenly distributed, then add a ton of good cracks of black pepper. Serve immediately with lemon wedges for squeezing.

## PARTY TRICK

- If you're making this ahead, wrap the lettuce in dry paper towels and pack in a large zip top bag. The croutons and dressing can travel in separate airtight containers. The Parmesan can stay in its wrapper and the lemons can be sliced at the gathering. Don't forget your serving bowl!

Parmesan
Round, 146

Herby
Challah,
124

# Pickled Potato Salad

ROLL UP YOUR SLEEVES | VG, GF, NF (V)

I'm Irish, so if you put a potato in front of me, I'm going to love it. But if you put a potato salad in front of me, I do have this short list of requests right here: lots of acid (that will always work in your favor), a little bit of heat (never a bad idea), fresh herb-iness (a reliable balance to starchy), and a hard no to raw onions stinking up the bowl. If you've been dying to have a killer potato salad in your arsenal—and really, everyone should—this recipe will help get you on the right track.

## Serves 6 to 8

3 pounds baby creamer potatoes (that's two 24-ounce bags), preferably in a mix of red, yellow, and purple

1 tablespoon plus 1 teaspoon kosher salt

1 cup dill pickles plus ¼ cup pickle brine, store-bought or homemade (page 54)

10 pepperoncini plus 2 tablespoons pepperoncini brine

2 tablespoons white wine vinegar

½ teaspoon celery seeds

1 bunch chives

1 cup mayonnaise (see Party Tricks)

2 tablespoons grainy mustard or spicy brown mustard

1 teaspoon freshly ground black pepper

½ cup loosely packed fresh parsley leaves, plus more for garnish

½ cup loosely packed fresh dill fronds, plus more for garnish

In a large Dutch oven, combine the potatoes, 1 tablespoon of the salt, and 8 cups cold water. Set over high heat and bring to a boil, about 10 minutes. Once bubbles are starting to pop all over the surface, set a timer for 8 minutes. When the timer goes off, use a spoon to remove a couple potatoes; if a paring knife slides in and right back out with no effort, you're good to go. If not, give them 2 more minutes before testing again.

Drain the potatoes, but don't rinse. Let them sit for about 5 minutes until you can comfortably cut them in half. Throw the halved potatoes in a large bowl and while they're still warm, toss with the pickle brine, the pepperoncini brine, vinegar, celery seeds, and the remaining 1 teaspoon salt. Let the potatoes cool completely and absorb those flavors, about 1 hour.

When the potatoes are cool, finely chop the pickles, pepperoncini, and chives. Add them to the bowl with the mayonnaise, grainy mustard, and black pepper and fold everything together. Add the parsley and dill and lightly toss to mix.

Pile the potato salad in a serving bowl, then garnish with more parsley and dill before serving.

## PARTY TRICKS

- A simple swap to vegan mayo makes this 100% plant-based.

- If you're making this ahead, cover with plastic wrap and refrigerate for up to 2 days. (Not a bad idea, the flavor only gets better over time.) Let it sit, covered, at room temperature for 30 minutes before serving. Wrap some herb leaves in damp paper towels and bring them along for garnish.

# Herb Salad
# with Homemade Ranch

IN YOUR SLEEP | VG, GF, NF

Let's not beat around the bush, this is really a recipe for ranch disguised as a salad. But if we're going to roll out the carpet for our queen, it's going to be the best carpet she's ever set foot on. Lightly seasoned breadcrumbs are always a good idea when you need a crunchy something on your salad and I consider whole herb leaves to be just as valid as the next salad green, but with a more exciting, distinctive flavor. If all you're hearing is blah blah blah, you can ignore all of this and mainline the ranch, I 100% understand.

**Serves 6 to 8**

**RANCH**
½ cup sour cream
½ cup mayonnaise
2 tablespoons buttermilk
  (see Party Tricks)
2 tablespoons thinly sliced fresh
  chives, or 1 tablespoon dried
2 tablespoons finely chopped
  fresh dill, or 1 tablespoon dried
2 tablespoons finely chopped
  fresh parsley, or 1 tablespoon
  dried
1 teaspoon kosher salt
1 teaspoon onion powder
½ teaspoon garlic powder
½ teaspoon freshly ground
  black pepper

**SALAD**
1 cup panko breadcrumbs
1 tablespoon extra-virgin
  olive oil
1 teaspoon smoked paprika
½ teaspoon kosher salt
2 romaine hearts
1 cup packed fresh dill fronds
1 cup packed fresh parsley
  leaves
1 cup packed fresh mint leaves

**Make the star of the show:** In a medium bowl, whisk the sour cream, mayonnaise, buttermilk, chives, dill, parsley, salt, onion powder, garlic powder, and pepper. It can be served right away, but, like all good things, it gets better as it sits. Transfer to an airtight container and refrigerate for up to 2 days. (This makes 1½ cups of dressing.)

**Make the supporting player:** In a small skillet, stir the panko and olive oil together. Set over low heat and toast, stirring occasionally, until lightly browned, about 3 minutes. Pull it off the stove and immediately stir in the paprika and salt. Set aside to cool.

Lay a romaine heart on a cutting board. Slice lengthwise, starting at the top and stopping just before the root. Flip the heart a quarter turn and slice lengthwise again, stopping before the root. Now cut across in 1-inch pieces, stopping just before the root, for perfectly bite-size lettuce. Do it all over again with the other heart. Now do everyone a favor and wash that lettuce in cold water and dry it well.

When it's time to assemble, toss the romaine, dill, parsley, mint, and about ½ cup of the dressing in a large bowl until everything is fully coated. Take a taste and decide if you need another tablespoon of dressing. Use your hands to scatter the salad on a large serving platter, fluffing the greens to give them plenty of height. Sprinkle the breadcrumbs over top. Serve the rest of the dressing on the side for drizzling.

## PARTY TRICKS

- Buttermilk is ideal here, if you have it. Otherwise, use another 1 tablespoon of sour cream with 1 tablespoon of white wine vinegar. Or, if you think homemade ranch might become a habit, buy a container of powdered buttermilk.

- If you're making this ahead, wrap the lettuce in dry paper towels, wrap the herbs in damp paper towels, and pack everything in a large zip top bag. The breadcrumbs and dressing can travel in separate airtight containers. Don't forget your serving platter!

# Shrimp Cocktail Ceviche

ROLL UP YOUR SLEEVES | GF, NF

Just when you thought there could not be anything more chic than a bowl of shrimp cocktail at a party, along comes Mexico, saying I can do you one better and offering up cóctel de camarón. This ceviche-influenced spin, with lightly poached shrimp swimming in a tomato sauce spiked with ketchup, plenty of lime, some crisp veg, and you already know there's hot sauce in there, is absolute perfection. The traditional serving vessel is a saltine, which is so gorgeous I could cry.

**Serves 6**

Kosher salt
Ice
1 pound frozen peeled shrimp
  (large, or around 26 to 30 per
  pound)
1 cup Clamato
½ cup ketchup
¼ cup fresh lime juice (from
  3 to 4 limes)
2 teaspoons freshly ground
  black pepper
2 teaspoons Mexican hot
  sauce, such as Valentina
4 Persian or mini cucumbers,
  diced
1 medium red onion, diced
¼ cup chopped fresh cilantro
Saltines, for serving

In a large saucepan, whisk 4 cups water and 1 tablespoon salt. Set over high heat and bring to a boil. Remove from the heat and immediately add the frozen shrimp. Cover and set a timer for 5 minutes. While the shrimp are poaching, fill a large bowl halfway with ice water and another 1 tablespoon salt. When the timer goes off, check a few shrimp to make sure they're fully opaque. (Back in for 1 minute if they're not!) Use a spider strainer or slotted spoon to transfer the shrimp to the ice bath and chill for about 5 minutes until they're completely cool. Now is a really great time to chop your cucumber and onion.

Drain the shrimp and remove the tails if they're not already off. Wash and dry the large ice bath bowl. She's coming back. Pat the shrimp dry with paper towels, then chop each shrimp crosswise into thirds.

In a medium serving bowl, whisk the Clamato, ketchup, lime juice, pepper, and hot sauce. Fold in the shrimp, cucumbers, and onion. Taste for seasoning—there's a rumor going around that I like to add about ¼ teaspoon of salt to help wake everything up, I don't know how that started. Cover the bowl tightly with plastic wrap and refrigerate for at least 2 hours or up to 24 hours. Just before serving, freshly chop the cilantro and fold in.

Load up that large bowl with ice and set the serving bowl inside it to keep the shrimp nice and cold. Serve with open sleeves of saltines to spoon on little cracker bites.

## PARTY TRICK

- If you're making this ahead, wrap the cilantro in damp paper towels. The saltines and shrimp cocktail are ready to go. Bring the large bowl along or ask your host if they have one (plus some ice) you can borrow.

# Fried Halloumi Caprese

IN YOUR SLEEP | VG, GF, NF

As in the panzanella (page 86), I'm going to ask, but not demand, that you wait for peak tomatoes. This salad is especially bare bones, so everything needs to be on point for it to sing. But when it's right, it's right. I love Halloumi in a caprese because (and this is not mozzarella slander) it has a sharper, saltier, tangy flavor and fries up so nicely for a slightly crispy outside. Flash frying fresh oregano not only crisps up the leaves, but also gives you a super fragrant oil to drizzle over the final salad.

## Serves 6

3 pounds ripe heirloom
   tomatoes
Flaky sea salt
16 ounces Halloumi cheese
1 tablespoon sesame seeds
½ cup extra-virgin olive oil
½ cup fresh oregano leaves
   (picked from 1 large bunch)
¼ cup fresh lemon juice (from
   1 to 2 lemons)
Freshly ground black pepper

Use a serrated knife to cut the tomatoes into ½-inch-thick slices. Transfer the pieces and any juices to a deep serving plate (to accumulate all those good juices) and blanket them with flaky salt. If you don't have flaky salt, just use what you have around. But salt those tomatoes well! Let them sit while working on the rest of the salad.

Use the serrated knife to slice the Halloumi as thin as you can, around ¼-inch pieces. Set those aside for a second. Spread the sesame seeds in a large nonstick skillet and set over low heat. Toss or stir constantly until the seeds are fragrant and slightly toasted, about 3 minutes. Pour them into a small bowl and set aside. Set the skillet back over low heat and add the olive oil and oregano leaves. Wiggle the skillet as the oregano fries until crisp, 30 seconds to 1 minute. Pour the oil and leaves into another small bowl to cool.

Put the skillet back over low heat one more time. (No need to add oil, the skillet is nicely coated from the oregano.) Working in batches, lay the Halloumi slices around the skillet without touching. Fry for 2 to 3 minutes on each side until they're beautifully golden brown. Use a fork to move the Halloumi to the tomato plate to cool while frying the rest.

Once the Halloumi is cool enough to touch, start working on an overlapping pattern of tomato and Halloumi. When that's to your satisfaction, spoon the oil and oregano over top, then drizzle the lemon juice all around. Sprinkle the sesame seeds and finish with a really generous amount of pepper before serving.

### PARTY TRICK
- If you're taking this to go, make it just before leaving the house and cover with plastic wrap until you get there. It's totally fine to let it sit—the juices will only improve with time—but don't refrigerate.

*White Beans +
Tinned Fish, 33*

Oil + Vin

Pesto

Red
Sauce

# Perfect Pasta Salad

ROLL UP YOUR SLEEVES | VG, NF

I could write an entire book about pasta salad, I just think it's so perfect. Pasta is the blankest canvas for whatever you want—for evidence, please see one million pasta dishes everywhere—so I really don't think there is a wrong answer here. But I do need to take a moment of your time to speak *my* truth about pasta salad. It often has cherry tomatoes and they're rarely good ones. It usually has raw red onion, which is immediately too pungent 3 seconds after dicing (my full rant is on page 90). It usually has a chopped herb of some kind that just withers into brownness as it sits. And most people fumble the best window of flavor by not letting the hot pasta soak in the flavors of the sauce! To all these ends, I've made three sauces that hit the mark for my dream salad: a spicy red sauce made with broiled cherry tomatoes, an Italian sub–inspired dressing made with lightly pickled red onions, and a quick little pesto for a vibrantly green chopped herb. And you better believe all three versions get tossed with the pasta hot out of the pot so the noodles can slightly soften and extremely saturate.

**Serves 6**

Pasta Sauce (see chart,
 page 82)
Kosher salt
12 to 16 ounces dried pasta in
 a fun shape, such as fusilli,
 gemelli, orecchiette, radiatori,
 or rigatoni
8 ounces mozzarella pearls,
 drained
4 ounces sliced salami, cut into
 ¼-inch strips (optional)
1 cup lightly packed fresh basil
 leaves
1 cup lightly packed fresh
 parsley leaves
½ cup sliced kalamata olives
½ cup sliced banana peppers,
 hot or mild
2 ounces Parmesan cheese

Make your pasta sauce and keep it close by. In a large Dutch oven, combine 12 cups water and 1 tablespoon salt. Set over high heat and bring to a boil. Stir in the pasta and cook until just al dente, according to the directions on the box. Drain in a colander and give it a few good shakes to get the water out.

In a large bowl, toss the pasta with about a third of the sauce. (Just eyeball it, it's all going in there eventually anyway.) Let the pasta sit for about 15 minutes to cool down. Then add any combo of the mozzarella, salami, basil, parsley, olives, and peppers and toss to combine. I need all of them to function, but this is your salad. Finally, toss in the last of the sauce. Cover the bowl tightly with plastic wrap and refrigerate for at least 2 hours or up to 24 hours—the flavor really improves the longer the ingredients mingle. Let it sit at room temperature, covered, for 30 minutes before serving. My only request is to save the Parm until just before serving and use a vegetable peeler to shave it directly into the bowl. Toss lightly, but mostly leave it on top.

*Recipe continues*

## PASTA SAUCE

| | |
|---|---|
| **RED SAUCE** | Preheat the oven to 500°F. In an 8 by 8-inch baking pan or oven-safe skillet, stir together 10 ounces whole cherry or grape tomatoes, 8 sun-dried tomatoes that have been finely chopped, ¼ cup extra-virgin olive oil, 2 grated garlic cloves, 1 tablespoon red wine vinegar, 1 tablespoon tomato paste, an optional 1 tablespoon Calabrian chile paste if you like it spicy, 1 teaspoon sugar, 1 teaspoon kosher salt, and ½ teaspoon freshly ground black pepper. Broil until the tomatoes are bursting, about 6 minutes. |
| **OIL + VIN** | In a medium bowl, combine ½ of a medium red onion that's been *very* thinly sliced, 2 grated garlic cloves, and ¼ cup red wine vinegar. Let the onions soak for 5 minutes to soften. Whisk in ¼ cup extra-virgin olive oil, ¼ cup mayonnaise, 1 teaspoon dried oregano, 1 teaspoon kosher salt, and 1 teaspoon freshly ground black pepper. |
| **PESTO** | In a food processor, combine 2 cups baby spinach, 1 cup fresh basil leaves, ⅓ cup pine nuts or walnuts, 2 ice cubes, the juice of 1 lemon, 2 grated garlic cloves, either 2 teaspoons white miso or 1 teaspoon kosher salt, and 1 teaspoon freshly ground black pepper. Process until the ice cubes stop rattling around and everything is nicely chopped. Add ½ cup extra-virgin olive oil and pulse 2 times just to combine. |

# Waldorf Salad with Poppy Dressing

ROLL UP YOUR SLEEVES | VG, GF

Even timeless things deserve fresh eyes once in a while. Waldorf salad, joining us all the way from the Gilded Age two centuries ago, definitely could be dusted off a little. I like to go all green with the veg and fruit, for a certain austere feeling. I also like hunks of salty blue cheese to break things up, and we might as well toast the walnuts too. Then, instead of a standard mayo dressing, I like a tangy, sweet, creamy poppy seed dressing to bring it all together.

**Serves 8**

**POPPY DRESSING**
1 tablespoon poppy seeds
¼ cup mayonnaise
¼ cup red wine vinegar
3 tablespoons honey
2 tablespoons Dijon mustard
½ teaspoon kosher salt

**SALAD**
2 cups walnuts
6 large celery stalks
2 Granny Smith apples
Juice of 1 lemon
2 cups seedless green grapes
8 ounces blue Stilton cheese

**Make the dressing:** In a small skillet, spread out the poppy seeds. Set over low heat, shaking the skillet often, until the poppy seeds smell nutty, about 2 minutes. Pour them into a small airtight container and whisk in the mayonnaise, vinegar, honey, mustard, and salt. Cover and refrigerate until ready to use, or for up to 2 days. This makes ¾ cup.

**Make the salad:** While that skillet is out anyway, add the walnuts and set over low heat. There will be more walnuts than surface area, so keep flipping or stirring constantly so everything can have some time in the hot seat. When you can really smell the walnuts toasting, pour them into a small bowl to cool.

Use a chef's knife to trim the tops and bottoms off the celery stalks (save the leaves if there are any!). Set a mandoline (see Party Tricks) over a medium serving bowl and hold each celery stalk at a 45-degree angle while slicing into long triangles. Stand the apples upright and cut them into four pieces around the core, then run each piece over the mandoline to make thin slices. Juice the lemon directly into the bowl and toss to coat the apples especially so they don't brown. Cut the grapes in half and add to the bowl. Roughly chop the walnuts and scrape them in. Crumble in the cheese, and if there were any celery leaves, pick them off and add them in whole.

Just before serving, add the dressing and toss to fully coat the salad.

## PARTY TRICKS

- When you're using a mandoline, it's not a bad idea to wear a clean, thick glove to protect your working hand. If you don't have one, using a zip-top bag as a glove is a great plan B. No matter what, take your time and pay attention, that blade is sharp. If you don't have a mandoline, just use a sharp chef's knife to thinly slice the celery.

- If you're packing this to go, make the salad just before walking out the door. Cover the bowl with plastic wrap, pack the dressing separately, and toss when you get there.

# Bagel Panzanella

ROLL UP YOUR SLEEVES | V, GF, NF

Don't even *think* about making this out of season! I'm kidding, it's a free country, make it whenever you want. But just know that it is in fact worth waiting for high summer when tomatoes are so ripe they're about to explode. Instead of hunting for a big crusty loaf, I love to just chop up and toast some bagels for a perfect foundation. A mix of herbs and spices join, only to highlight what's already great about a panzanella: bread swimming in tomato juices.

**Serves 6 to 8**

6 sesame bagels, or everything or onion or whatever you love, gluten-free if you want
3 tablespoons extra-virgin olive oil
6 medium heirloom tomatoes
Flaky sea salt
1 large shallot, minced
2 big garlic cloves, grated
½ teaspoon cumin seeds
½ teaspoons caraway seeds
½ teaspoon fennel seeds (see Party Tricks)
1 tablespoon red wine vinegar
½ cup loosely packed fresh basil leaves
¼ cup loosely packed fresh parsley leaves

Preheat the oven to 450°F. Line a rimmed baking sheet with parchment paper.

Use a serrated knife to split the bagels and cut them into 1-inch pieces. Arrange on the baking sheet and toss with 2 tablespoons of the olive oil. Slide the baking sheet into the oven and set a timer for 5 minutes. Check to see if they're nicely toasted and maybe give them 2 more minutes.

While the bagels toast, use the serrated knife again to chop the tomatoes into 1-inch cubes. Pour the tomatoes and all their juices into a large bowl and blanket them with flaky salt to coax out all that good juice. If you don't have flaky salt, just use what you have around. But salt those tomatoes well!

In a small skillet, heat the remaining 1 tablespoon olive oil over low heat. When the oil easily glides across the skillet, add the shallot, garlic, cumin, caraway, and fennel seeds. Stir until everything is so fragrant you could die, about 1 minute. Immediately scrape that warm mixture over the tomatoes, add the vinegar, and toss. Add the bagel pieces, basil, and parsley and toss again.

## PARTY TRICKS

- Cumin, caraway, and fennel are my holy trinity, but if you only have one or two of the three, that's okay, too!

- This really should be made just before leaving the house. Pack the toasted bagel pieces, basil, and parsley separately in an airtight container so you can toss them in when you get there.

Maple-Miso
Smashed
Cucumbers, 89

# Maple-Miso Smashed Cucumbers

IN YOUR SLEEP | V, GF, NF

Crisp, juicy cukes drowning in a salty, acidic, spicy dressing. As the great Hilary Duff once said, "This is what dreams are made of." My version plays with a maple-miso mixture (better friends than you would expect!) that adds a nice hint of sweetness while still letting everything else come to the front. I also—controversy alert!—like to scoop out my cucumbers; cucumbers are 90 percent water and a lot of that moisture is concentrated in the seed area, so a quick scoop helps keep the sauce from diluting too much over time. If it's hot out and the grill is on, this is absolutely coming with me.

**Serves 4**

1 pound Persian or mini cucumbers
1 tablespoon kosher salt
3 tablespoons rice vinegar
3 tablespoons pure maple syrup
2 tablespoons white miso paste
1 teaspoon sesame oil
¼ teaspoon red pepper flakes
2 tablespoons toasted sesame seeds

Slice the cucumbers in half lengthwise and use a soup spoon to scrape the seeds out. It doesn't need to be perfect, just enough to help cut down on liquid. Lay the cucumbers cut side down and use a rolling pin or meat tenderizer (or even a can of beans) to lightly smash them. Not so hard that they break apart, just enough to make good cracks. Use a chef's knife to roughly chop them in 1-inch pieces.

In a medium bowl, toss the cucumbers with the salt and 1 tablespoon of the vinegar. Cover with a kitchen towel and set a timer for 30 minutes. By the time you come back the cucumbers should have released a lot of water. Drain them thoroughly and wipe the bowl clean.

In the same bowl, whisk the remaining 2 tablespoons vinegar, plus the maple syrup, miso, sesame oil, and red pepper flakes. Add the cucumbers and toss to coat. Just before serving, sprinkle the sesame seeds over the top.

## PARTY TRICK
- If you're making this ahead, wait to drain the cucumbers and toss in the dressing until right before you head out the door.

# Black Bean Salad with Sazón Vinaigrette

IN YOUR SLEEP | V, GF, NF

One of my big motivations for writing this book, and especially this chapter, is my crusade to never have to eat a raw onion in a salad ever again. I simply hate feeling like my esophagus is under attack. So if there's one thing this recipe teaches you—and empowers you to immediately adapt as a credo—it's this: there's always time for a quick pickle. Letting these veggies mingle with some acid for a few minutes mellows their harsh edge, brightens their natural colors, and builds flavor for the very liquid that is about to become a savory Sazón dressing, an ideal partner to a bean salad if there ever was one. When we can let the flavors sing together, we all win! I love the dense texture of black beans as a base here, but any of your favorite canned beans can slide right in.

**Serves 8**

½ cup rice wine vinegar or white wine vinegar
Juice of 4 limes
2 teaspoons kosher salt
1 jalapeño, diced (I like seeds, but see Party Tricks on page 35 to remove them)
8 sweet mini peppers, diced
½ medium red onion, diced
4 scallions, thinly sliced
2 ripe avocados, halved, pitted, and diced (see Party Tricks on page 24 for nailing ripe ones)
2 (15.5-ounce) cans black beans, drained and rinsed
¼ cup chopped fresh cilantro leaves and stems
2 tablespoons vegetable oil
2 packets Sazón seasoning, any flavor (see Party Trick)
1 teaspoon freshly ground black pepper

In a medium serving bowl, whisk the vinegar, lime juice, salt, and ¼ cup of cold water. As you dice the jalapeño, peppers, onion, scallions, and avocado, add them to the bowl and lightly toss to coat in the vinegar mixture. Set a timer for 10 minutes to lightly pickle.

Add the black beans, cilantro, vegetable oil, and Sazón. Toss to completely mix, then taste for seasoning. Serve immediately, or cover the bowl tightly with plastic wrap and refrigerate for up to 2 days. Stir again before serving.

## PARTY TRICK

- Sazón is a pan-Latin pantry staple, made from vibrantly colored annatto, turmeric, or saffron mixed with fragrant spices like coriander, cumin, garlic, or oregano. The magic ingredient is MSG, which gives this salad irresistible umami. If you're using a bottle of Sazón instead of packets, measure out ½ tablespoon per packet. You could also use an equal amount of Tajín or a chili powder mix instead and adjust the salt as needed.

# THANKS A BRUNCH

**AT A CERTAIN AGE**—and maybe you're not there yet, but trust me, you will be one day—battling hungover hordes for a table and equally hungover waiters for a mimosa refill just isn't worth it. But brunching at home should still feel buzzy and exciting. These fun drinks, sweets, and savories will help keep the energy up. The best part of this chapter is everything can be started or fully made a day ahead. So no matter what happened the night before, at least your dish will be looking fresh-faced and flawless!

# Dirty Horchata

*Start this recipe 1 day ahead.*

Horchata, an absolutely perfect Mexican drink made from rice and cinnamon, needs no dressing up. But just say—let's just imagine here—that you were going to add one more thing to go with it. Wouldn't a splash of cold brew be the most wonderful iced coffee you've ever had in your life? This recipe lets you have it both ways. Follow it exactly as-is and hold the coffee for a classic horchata or dirty it up with some caffeine for the best possible start to the day.

**Serves 8**

2 cups long-grain white rice
2 thick cinnamon sticks, or
  1 tablespoon ground cinnamon
1 (14-ounce) can sweetened
  condensed milk
2 (12-ounce) cans evaporated
  milk
Ice
1 (32-ounce) bottle cold brew
  concentrate

Combine the rice and cinnamon sticks with 3 cups water in a medium saucepan. Set over high heat and bring to a boil. Remove from the heat, cover, and set a timer for 2 hours so the saucepan can cool down, then refrigerate overnight to soak the rice.

Pour the rice, cinnamon sticks, and any liquid into a blender and add the sweetened condensed milk. Blend on high until completely smooth, about 2 minutes. Set a mesh strainer over a pitcher that can hold at least 8 cups (64 ounces) and pour the horchata through, stopping to stir as needed to help the liquid pass through. Stir in the cans of evaporated milk. Cover the pitcher with plastic wrap and keep chilled until it's party time, or up to 24 hours. Give it a good stir again before serving.

When it's time, fill a 16-ounce cup halfway with ice. Add ½ cup of cold brew to the cup and top with 1 cup of horchata. (Or skip the coffee and just fill her up with horchata!)

# Orange Cantaloupe Agua Fresca

ROLL UP YOUR SLEEVES | V, GF, NF, NA

Basically sunshine in a glass, this light and refreshing agua fresca is the perfect OJ-adjacent drink for blurring the line between morning and afternoon. The only essential step is making sure your cantaloupe is perfectly ripe. Knocking is the old stand by, but do you really know what you're listening for? Look for one that's surprisingly heavy, nicely beige with some green undertones, sweet and floral when you sniff the stem, and firm all over with just a little give at that stem area.

**Serves 6 to 12**

1 (4- to 5-pound) ripe cantaloupe
2 medium navel oranges
2 medium limes
¼ to ½ cup sugar
Ice

Cut the cantaloupe in half and use a soup spoon to scrape out and discard the seeds. Hold one of the cantaloupe halves over a blender and use the spoon to scoop chunks of flesh into the blender. Add 1 cup water and blend the cantaloupe on high until completely smooth, about 2 minutes. Set a mesh strainer over a pitcher that can hold at least 8 cups (64 ounces) and pour the cantaloupe juice through, stopping to stir as needed to help the liquid pass through. Repeat with the other cantaloupe half and another 1 cup water.

Peel the oranges (some white pith is fine), break into segments, and toss them in the blender. Juice the limes into the blender and then add ¼ cup sugar. Pour about 1 cup of the cantaloupe juice into the blender (you can eyeball this, it doesn't need to be exact) and blend on high until the oranges are completely broken down, about 2 minutes. Pour through the strainer and then give the pitcher a good stir to combine all the juices. Take a taste for sweetness. If you think it needs more sugar, add another ¼ cup and stir really well until it's dissolved. Cover the pitcher with plastic wrap and keep chilled until it's party time, or up to 24 hours. Give it a good stir before serving.

### PARTY TRICK

- There are two paths to take for serving here. The first path is to pack a 16-ounce cup with ice, fill with the agua fresca, and slide a straw in. The second path is to fill a Champagne glass halfway with the juice and top off with Champagne, or a Champagne to juice ratio that feels good to each brunch monster in that moment.

Dirty Horchata,
95

Orange Cantaloupe
Agua Fresca, 96

Dirty Horchata,
95

# The Best Bloody

ROLL UP YOUR SLEEVES | GF, NF (V, NA)

Call me crazy, but I love sipping a cold Bloody Mary mix even without the booze. (The gap between bloody and gazpacho is razor-thin, if you think about it.) Everyone has their own likes and dislikes, but the blender mix of tomato, roasted pepper, and celery is the key foundation to get some vegetal umami base going, and you can wiggle around the seasonings to fit your taste from there. The mix only gets better with some fridge time so make it the night before when you know you'll need it the morning after.

**Serves 10**

1 (28-ounce) can whole peeled tomatoes
1 (12-ounce) jar roasted red peppers
2 large celery stalks
½ cup pickle brine
¼ cup fresh lemon juice (from 2 lemons)
1 tablespoon prepared horseradish
1 tablespoon Worcestershire sauce (see Party Tricks)
1 tablespoon tamari or fish sauce
1 teaspoon freshly ground black pepper
1 teaspoon hot sauce
2 cups lemon vodka, preferably Absolut Citron (see Party Tricks)
Ice, celery stalks, and lemon wedges, for serving

In a blender, pour in the entire can of tomatoes, liquid and all. Drain the liquid out of the pepper jar, then add them to the blender. Roughly chop the celery and add to the blender, along with the pickle brine. Blend on high until completely smooth, about 2 minutes.

Pour the mix into a pitcher that can hold at least 8 cups (64 ounces) and add the lemon juice, horseradish, Worcestershire, tamari, black pepper, and hot sauce. Cover the pitcher with plastic wrap and keep chilled until it's party time, or up to 3 days. Stir in the vodka just before go time.

Fill a 16-ounce cup to the top with ice and pour in the bloody. Use a celery stalk to stir and perch a lemon wedge on the rim before serving.

## PARTY TRICKS

- This is on a strictly need-to-know basis, but Worcestershire sauce is made with anchovies. If you want a vegetarian/vegan-friendly mix, buy a vegan Worcestershire or just double up on the tamari. Me, I like to get wild and do a Worcestershire + fish sauce combo.

- Swap in 2 cups blanco tequila for a Bloody Maria or leave out the alcohol altogether for a Virgin Mary.

# A Triflin' Parfait

IN YOUR SLEEP | VG, NF (GF)

Do you know the difference between a trifle and a parfait? Yeah, I'm not sure either. Either way, it's a delicious pile of something creamy, something fruity, and something carby. In this case, we're really taking the easy way out with a fully store-bought list of ingredients, carefully assembled for the illusion of hours of work. The dairy element is a tangy-sweet mix of cream cheese and sour cream whipped with cream, powdered sugar, and maple syrup. Frozen berries perked up with the juice and zest of an orange thaw into a juicy fruity layer. For the carby, it's dual layers of cut-up pound cake (dream) and crushed up gingersnaps (twist) to make sure this parfait is triflin' in name only. (But maybe it *is* a trifle? I'm still not sure.)

## Serves 6

1 (14- to 16-ounce) box gingersnaps (see Party Trick)
1 (8-ounce) block cream cheese, cubed
2 cups sour cream
2 cups heavy cream
1 cup powdered sugar
2 tablespoons pure maple syrup
2 store-bought pound cakes, cut into ½-inch cubes (see Party Trick)
1 (16-ounce bag) frozen berries
1 navel orange

### SPECIAL EQUIPMENT
3-quart (96-ounce) trifle bowl

Put the gingersnaps in a large zip-top bag. Use a rolling pin or meat tenderizer or a can of beans to smash into fine crumbs. (Or pulse in a food processor 6 to 8 times.)

In a large bowl, combine the sour cream and cream cheese. Use a handheld mixer to beat on low until the cream cheese is mostly broken up. Add the cream, powdered sugar, and maple syrup and beat on low until the sugar is combined, then crank up to medium and beat to stiff peaks, about 3 minutes. (This can also be done using a stand mixer fitted with the whisk attachment.)

Last bit of prep, I promise! Open the bag of frozen fruit and zest the orange right into the bag. Slice the orange in half and squeeze the juice in there, too. Hold the bag closed and give it a good shake to mix.

Okay, we're ready to build. Layer a third of the cake cubes on the bottom of a 3-quart trifle bowl or similarly sized glass bowl and press gently to squish them down a little. Add a third of the whipped cream, a third of the gingersnap crumbs, and 1 cup of the frozen berries. Another layer of cake, then whipped cream, gingersnaps, berries, and do it all once more to use everything up. Lightly drape plastic wrap over the top of the bowl and refrigerate for at least 1 hour so the berries can thaw, or up to 12 hours.

### PARTY TRICK
- Biscoff, Nilla Wafers, Maria cookies, graham crackers, any shortbread cookie, or a gluten-free replacement all work. Sara Lee's 16-ounce pound cake (thawed) or Entenmann's loaf cake both work great, as do any of your gluten-free favorites.

# Cream-Soaked Cinnamon Rolls

BRAGGING RIGHTS | VG, NF

*Optional: Start this recipe 1 day ahead.*

Not to be dramatic, but these are the softest rolls you'll ever eat. Every single bite is like that perfectly soft center bite, which is how life should be. The pillowy dough has milk powder— my secret weapon for extra-soft pastry—and the entire pan of rolls gets bathed in cream before baking so all the fat can soak in for an almost-brioche texture. The bad news is there is no cream cheese frosting. The incredible news is that it's because the cream cheese is *inside* the rolls, which is maybe where it should have been the entire time. Adding a little tang helps break up the sweet richness and the slow-melting action means a super gooey filling.

**Makes 12 rolls**

## DOUGH
½ cup (1 stick) unsalted butter
1 cup (230 grams) whole milk
4 cups (560 grams) all-purpose flour
¼ cup (40 grams) milk powder
2 tablespoons granulated sugar
1 teaspoon baking powder
1 (0.25-ounce) packet instant yeast (see Party Tricks)
1 large egg
1½ teaspoons kosher salt
Nonstick cooking spray

## FILLING
1 (8-ounce) block cream cheese
1 cup (215 grams) dark brown sugar
2 tablespoons ground cinnamon
¼ teaspoon kosher salt
½ cup heavy cream

## FROSTING
2½ cups (300 grams) powdered sugar
3 to 5 tablespoons whole milk

## SPECIAL EQUIPMENT
Stand mixer

**Make the dough:** In a small microwave-safe bowl, combine the butter and milk. Microwave on high in 30-second bursts just until the butter is melted. It'll probably take 60 to 90 seconds, but everyone's microwave is different. (This can also be done in a small saucepan over low heat, then poured into a small bowl to cool slightly.) Carefully—CAREFULLY!—dip a knuckle in to test the mixture. It should be warm but not hot, and if it's hot let it sit until it's warm.

In the bowl of a stand mixer fitted with the dough hook, combine the flour, milk powder, granulated sugar, baking powder, and yeast. Mix on low speed for a couple of seconds to combine. With the mixer running on low, slowly stream in the milk mixture. Crack the egg into the small bowl you just emptied, then side it into the flour. (No eggshells on my watch!) Once the flour is mostly hydrated, add the salt, move up to medium speed, and set a timer for 5 minutes. Let the hook battle it out until the sides of the bowl are pretty clean and the dough is lifting up from the bottom. It should be smooth, soft, and maybe a little sticky but not overly so.

Coat a large bowl with nonstick spray, then scrape the dough into the bowl. Cover the bowl tightly with plastic wrap and set in a warm place to proof (see Party Tricks). Set a timer for 1 hour and take a second right now to set the cream cheese out to soften. Enjoy your break—by the time you come back, the dough should be beautifully puffy and doubled in size.

Coat a 9 by 13-inch baking pan with nonstick spray. Discard the plastic and punch down the dough. The dough should be barely sticky, so it's fine to go right onto the counter. (If you're having trouble with too much sticking, scoop the dough up and spritz the counter with nonstick spray.) Roll out the dough to a 14-inch square.

*Recipe continues*

**Make the filling:** Spread the cream cheese evenly over the dough, leaving a 1-inch border on all sides. In a small bowl, pinch the sugar, cinnamon, and salt together to mix, then sprinkle it evenly over the cream cheese. Starting with the edge closest to you, roll the dough up into a tight log. Flip it so the seam is facing up and very tightly pinch it closed along the length. Use a ruler and a serrated knife to score 14 marks 1-inch apart along the dough. Cut off 1-inch from either end of the dough and discard, then cut the dough into 12 pieces following the score marks. As you cut each swirl, arrange it in the baking pan making 4 rows of 3 evenly spaced out.

Spritz some tin foil with nonstick spray and cover the baking pan tightly. You have two options at this point. Set the baking pan somewhere warm (but not in the oven) for an hour to let the rolls rise until they're puffy and almost filling the dish, or move the baking pan to the refrigerator for up to 24 hours, then set it somewhere warm for 90 minutes.

While the rolls rise, preheat the oven to 375°F.

When the rolls are ready to bake, carefully peel back the foil and pour the cream into the bottom of the baking pan, doing your best to fill in the cracks while avoiding the rolls. Cover the dish with the foil and slide onto the lower rack. Set a timer for 15 minutes. Discard the foil and set a timer for 20 minutes, until the tops of the rolls are golden brown and the cream is mostly absorbed. (Any extra cream will soak in while cooling.) Cool in the pan for 30 minutes.

**While the rolls are still warm, make the frosting:** In a medium bowl, whisk the powdered sugar with 3 tablespoons of milk until it's hydrated. Continue whisking in milk 1 tablespoon at a time until you have a thick but spreadable frosting. Evenly spread it over the warm rolls. You can serve the rolls immediately or let them cool completely before serving.

## PARTY TRICKS

- I prefer instant yeast because—are you sitting down?—it's instant. It can get mixed right in with everything else, no head start needed, and gets to work much faster than active dry for shorter and more efficient proof times. Just make sure to always buy in small quantities, store in the fridge, and use within 3 months.

- Here's how to turn your oven into the perfect proofing box: Set the oven racks in the center and lower third. Slide a baking pan (any size) on the bottom rack. In a medium saucepan, set 4 cups water over high heat so it can get to a ripping boil. Set your covered dough on the center rack, pour the boiling water into the baking pan, and immediately shut the oven door. The hot steam is going to create the perfectly humid proofing environment. Just don't open that door until your timer goes off!

# Loaded Rösti

ROLL UP YOUR SLEEVES | GF, NF (V, VG)

Some might say watches, chocolate, or knives, but I would say rösti is the best thing to come out of Switzerland. If you're Swiss, don't read this next part—a rösti is like a supersized order of Denny's hash browns, shreds of potato perfectly crisp on the outside and so soft and tender on the inside. Usually, it's just lightly seasoned and fried, but potatoes are an excellent base for building flavor and I like the loaded baked potato feeling of crispy pancetta, melted cheddar, and a sour cream and chive topping (all optional). Every great brunch needs a great potato element, and this one not only travels beautifully but is equally delicious hot or room temp.

**Serves 6 to 8**

3 medium russet potatoes
4 ounces sharp cheddar cheese (see Party Tricks)
2 teaspoons freshly ground black pepper
1 teaspoon kosher salt
1 teaspoon onion powder
1 teaspoon garlic powder
1 (4-ounce) package diced pancetta
4 tablespoons extra-virgin olive oil
Sour cream, for serving
1 bunch chives, for serving

Wash the potatoes thoroughly under cold water (we're keeping the skins on, so we want them clean!). Lay a kitchen towel on the counter, then set a box grater in the center. Working with one at a time, grate each potato on the large holes of the grater (see Party Tricks). Stop when you need to, don't sacrifice a finger. Push the pile of grated potato off to the side before grating the next one. Gather up the corners of the towel so the potatoes clump at the bottom. Twist, twist, twist the top of the towel until it starts squeezing liquid out of the potatoes. Get as much as you can, but it doesn't have to be perfect.

Dump the grated potatoes into a medium bowl. Spread out the towel again and replace the box grater. Grate the cheese on the large holes, then shake into the bowl with the potato. Add the pepper, salt, onion powder, and garlic powder to the bowl. Use your hands to toss everything and coat the potato shreds.

Spread out the pancetta in a large nonstick skillet. Set over medium heat, using a rubber spatula to stir occasionally, until the fat has rendered and the pancetta is browned, about 6 minutes. Scrape the pancetta and fat into the potato mixture and use the spatula to mix.

Set the skillet back over medium heat, pour in 2 tablespoons of the olive oil, and tilt to coat the skillet. Use the spatula to scrape in the potato mixture and smooth into an even layer. Cover and set a timer for 5 minutes. Uncover and slide the spatula between the potatoes and skillet and slide it around the perimeter. Give the skillet a shake to make sure the rösti wiggles. If it's stuck, slide the spatula a little farther under and shake until it comes loose. Continue to cook, uncovered and occasionally wiggling, for another 6 or 7 minutes, until the edges are a deep brown.

*Recipe continues*

We're going to use two dinner plates here to flip. Make sure the rösti wiggles, then slide it out onto the first plate. Set the skillet back on the heat and add the remaining 2 tablespoons olive oil to heat up. Set the second plate over the rösti and flip so the browned side is now up. Tilt to coat the skillet, then quickly slide the rösti back in to brown the bottom. Cook, still uncovered, for another 8 minutes, until the bottom is equally browned. Keep sliding that spatula under and wiggling it around periodically.

Slide the rösti out of the skillet and onto a serving platter to cool for at least 10 minutes. If you're transporting it, drape a clean kitchen towel over the top so steam can still escape. The rösti can be served hot, warm, or room temperature. If you want to reheat it, slide it off the platter and onto a rimmed baking sheet and warm in a 300°F oven for 10 minutes. (Make sure to secure a baking sheet and oven space with your host ahead of time!)

Just before serving, cut the rösti in 6 or 8 pieces. Set out the sour cream so everyone can plop a dollop on their slice and pass around the chives with kitchen scissors to snip over top.


## PARTY TRICKS

- Lose the cheese and pancetta to make this vegan and serve with dairy-free sour cream. To make it vegetarian, skip the pancetta and heat the olive oil in the skillet until it glides when you tilt it.

- If you're a perfectionist, run the potatoes over a mandoline to make thin rounds, then stack the rounds in small piles and slice into thin strips.

# Radish + Seaweed Butter

IN YOUR SLEEP | V, GF, NF

I think there's a beauty in simplicity, and sometimes the easiest things make the biggest impression. This is as simple as it gets: Buy the freshest, most colorful radishes you can. Invest in really excellent butter, the kind you'd never buy for yourself. Find a great jar of nori. Take your time and get the chives very finely diced. Make sure the bread is top tier. And that's all you need for a sublimely delicious dish.

**Serves 4 to 6**

½ cup (1 stick) high-quality unsalted butter, or 8 tablespoons vegan butter
1 tablespoon nori flakes or furikake rice seasoning (see Party Tricks)
1 teaspoon kosher salt
1 tablespoon finely chopped fresh chives
2 bunches radishes, leaves on if that's an option
Store-bought baguette or Seeded Barbari (page 137)

Set out the butter to soften for around 45 minutes, or do the microwave trick (page 202). In a small bowl, use a fork to smash the softened butter, nori, and salt together.

Add the chives to the bowl and use the fork to smash them into the butter and mix everything together. Scrape the butter into a 4-ounce ramekin or use parchment paper to roll it into a rough log. If you're using it soon, keep it at room temperature. If not, wrap tightly in plastic wrap and refrigerate for up to 5 days, then bring to room temp before serving.

And speaking of serving, wash the radishes really well under cold water, then pat dry with a clean kitchen towel. If the leaves are pretty, leave them on. If they're a little wilted and brown, chop them off, leaving about 1 inch of stem. Cut each radish in half lengthwise. Arrange the radish halves on one side of a serving plate. Use a serrated knife to slice the baguette in thin rounds (cut the barbari into small squares, if that's your journey) and arrange on the other side of the plate. Set the butter in the center with a small cheese spreader or butter knife. Wrap the entire plate in plastic if you're traveling and serve when you get there.

## PARTY TRICKS

- Jars of nori flakes or furikake can usually be found in whichever aisle has soy sauce and sesame oil. Just be warned: furikake usually has dried fish in the mix!

- To keep the radishes extra crisp, and make brunch feel extra chic, arrange them in a bowl of ice.

# Gochujang + Cheddar Scones

ROLL UP YOUR SLEEVES | VG, NF

Gochujang, a sweet-savory-spicy Korean chile paste, is one of my most used pantry items because it improves just about any sauce, dip, or soup. It also happens to be the perfect accent in these scones, giving them a pretty orange hue and a ton of flavor that blends perfectly with cheddar and scallion for a really fresh POV on very familiar scones. And since I've already scandalized the Commonwealth, we might as well give these scones a very American makeover with layers of buttery flakiness for soft and tender bites.

**Makes 6 scones**

Nonstick cooking spray
2½ cups (350 grams) all-purpose flour
2 teaspoons baking powder
2 teaspoons kosher salt
1 cup (2 sticks) unsalted butter, very cold
2 cups (230 grams) shredded cheddar cheese (see Party Trick)
2 scallions, thinly sliced
½ cup (130 grams) buttermilk, very cold
3 tablespoons gochujang
1 large egg

## PARTY TRICK

- Usually it's ideal to shred your own cheese, but in this case we want the bag. It's coated in starch to prevent clumping, which also stops it from melting too fast and spilling out of the scone.

Preheat the oven to 400°F and set a rack in the upper third. Line a rimmed baking sheet with parchment paper. Spritz the large holes of a box grater with nonstick spray.

In a large bowl, whisk the flour, baking powder, and salt. Set the box grater over the bowl and grate all but 1 tablespoon of each stick of butter over the large holes. (Keep those 2 tablespoons of butter off to the side, we'll need them later!) Add the cheese and scallions and toss to fully coat in the flour mixture. Make a little well in the center and add the buttermilk, gochujang, and egg. Whisk until the wet ingredients are fully mixed, then switch to a spatula and stir to form a slightly sticky dough.

Lay a big piece of plastic wrap on the counter (I like to use cans of beans to hold the corners of my plastic in place) and place the dough in the center. Use wet hands to pat it into a roughly 8-inch square. Fold the square in thirds like a letter, then pat it back into an 8-inch square. Fold one more time, then pat into an 8-inch round. Cup one hand around the edge while the other hand presses on top and rotate around so the dough is nice and even. Wrap it up tight, set it on a large plate, and freeze for 15 minutes.

Melt the remaining 2 tablespoons butter on the stovetop or in the microwave. Unwrap the dough, set it in the center of the prepared baking sheet, and brush the top with the melted butter. Cut the dough into 6 equal triangles and space them out evenly across the sheet so they have room to grow. Bake on the upper rack for about 15 minutes, until golden brown and fluffy. Cool for 10 minutes on the baking sheet, then transfer to a wire rack to finish cooling. If you want to bring them warm, wrap them in a large kitchen towel after cooling on the rack for 15 minutes. They're equally excellent at room temp.

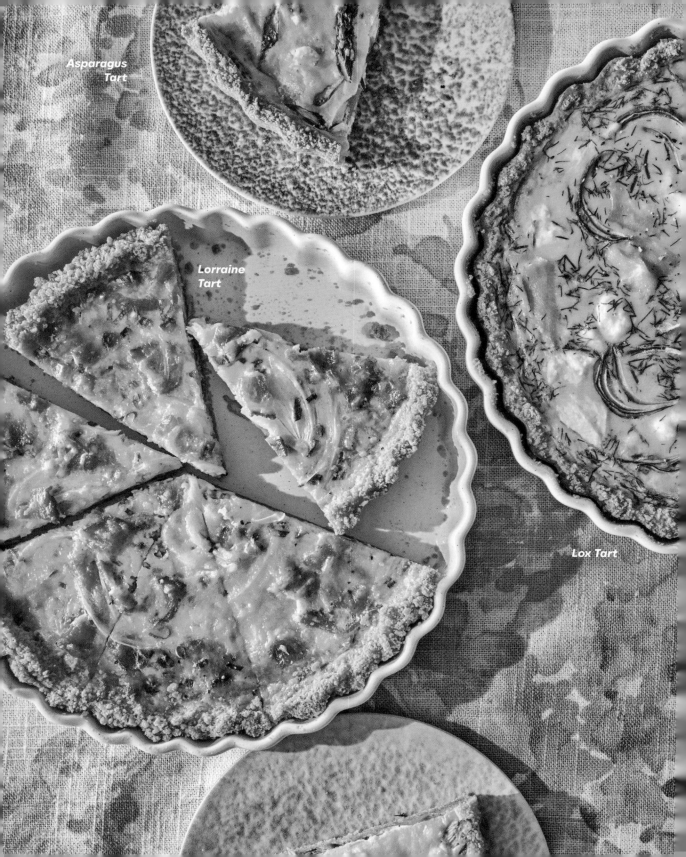

Asparagus
Tart

Lorraine
Tart

Lox Tart

# Cheesy Breakfast Tart

ROLL UP YOUR SLEEVES | VG, NF

Yes, it is technically a quiche, but that word is very silly and breakfast tart sounds so special. There's a choose-your-own-flavor-adventure element here, with three cheesy fillings centered around asparagus, smoked salmon, or bacon, depending on your mood. The nice thing here is that it's socially acceptable to serve a breakfast tart at any temperature: hot, cold, or anywhere in between. So make it ahead or bring it fresh. It truly doesn't matter!

**Serves 6**

Nonstick cooking spray

**CRUST**
2½ cups Cheez-Its (from a
   21-ounce box)
2 tablespoons unsalted butter,
   melted
1 large egg white (save the yolk
   for the filling!)

**FILLING**
2 large eggs plus 1 large egg
   yolk
½ cup whole milk
½ cup heavy cream
½ teaspoon kosher salt
½ teaspoon freshly ground
   black pepper
Mix-Ins (see chart below)

Preheat the oven to 375°F and set a rack in the center. Coat a 9-inch pie plate with nonstick spray and set on a rimmed baking sheet.

**Make the crust:** Put the crackers in a zip-top bag and use a rolling pin or meat tenderizer or a can of beans to lightly smash into fine crumbs. (Or pulse in a food processor 6 to 8 times.) In a large bowl, whisk the butter and egg white together. Use a spatula to fold the crumbs into butter mixture until they're completely coated. Scoop the cracker mixture into the greased pie plate and press evenly over the bottom and sides of the plate. Use a fork to prick all over the crust so it doesn't puff up too much. Slide the pie plate into the oven and set a timer for 10 minutes, until the crust is toasted and fragrant.

**While the crust is baking, make the filling:** In the same large bowl (no need to clean it), whisk the eggs, egg yolk, milk, cream, salt, and pepper together until there are no droopy streaks falling off your whisk. Fold in the Mix-Ins of your choosing, then pour into the crust. Bake for 30 to 35 minutes, until the filling is a little puffy and the center is just barely set. Cool for at least 30 minutes before slicing, or cool completely. The cooled tart can be wrapped in plastic and stored at room temperature for up to 2 days or refrigerated for up to 4 days. Serve hot, warm, room temp, or cold, it's all good!

| MIX-INS | | |
|---|---|---|
| **ASPARAGUS** | **LOX** | **LORRAINE** |
| • 4 ounces goat cheese, crumbled | • 4 ounces cream cheese, cubed | • 4 ounces Gruyère, shredded |
| • 12 asparagus spears, cut into ½-inch pieces | • 4 ounces smoked salmon, diced | • 8 slices thick-cut bacon, cooked and crumbled |
| • 1 small shallot, thinly sliced | • ½ medium red onion, thinly sliced | • ½ medium yellow onion, thinly sliced |
| • 2 tablespoons thinly sliced fresh chives | • 2 tablespoons chopped fresh dill | • 2 scallions, thinly sliced |

# Box of Donuts

BRAGGING RIGHTS | VG, NF

*Optional: Start this recipe 1 day ahead.*

Of all the possible things to bring, I think this is my favorite. Nothing will shoot you to the top of everyone's list faster than showing up with a box of freshly fried and glazed donuts, even still a little warm perhaps. But wait, doesn't making fresh donuts take a lot of time? You bet it does, bud! That's why you can break it up by making your dough the day before and frying your donuts the next morning (90 percent of that time is zoning out to TikTok while your dough rises, you've got this). For an extra-special touch, I like to nicely ask a local donut shop for a large box—they're always willing to slide one across the counter if you're willing to buy a couple treats—so I can literally arrive at brunch with a box of donuts.

## Makes a baker's dozen plus donut holes

### DONUTS
½ cup (1 stick) unsalted butter
1 cup (230 grams) whole milk
3½ cups (490 grams) all-
  purpose flour, plus more for
  rolling
6 tablespoons sugar
1 (0.25-ounce) packet instant
  yeast (see Party Tricks on
  page 104)
¼ teaspoon ground nutmeg
2 large eggs
1 teaspoon pure vanilla extract
1½ teaspoons kosher salt
Nonstick cooking spray
2 quarts vegetable oil

**Make the donuts:** In a small microwave-safe bowl, combine the butter and milk. Microwave on high in 30-second bursts just until the butter is melted. It'll take anywhere from 60 to 90 seconds or beyond, so keep checking. (This can also be done in a small saucepan over low heat, then poured into a small bowl to cool slightly.) Carefully—no, seriously, be careful—dip a knuckle in to test the mixture. It should be warm but not hot, and if it's hot let it sit until it's warm.

In the bowl of a stand mixer fitted with the dough hook, combine the flour, sugar, yeast, and nutmeg. Mix on low for a couple seconds to combine. Keep mixing and slowly stream in the milk mixture. Crack the eggs into the small bowl you just emptied, then pour them into the mixer with the vanilla, too. Once the flour is mostly hydrated, add the salt, move up to medium speed, and set a timer for 10 minutes. Lean on your stand mixer to hold it in place and scroll on your phone. When the timer goes off, the dough should be smooth and soft, and the bowl should be clean. (See Party Tricks.)

Coat a large bowl with nonstick spray, then scrape the dough into the bowl. Cover tightly with plastic wrap and make sure that perimeter is sealed tight. Put the bowl in a warm place to rise. (See Party Tricks on page 104 for the perfect spot.) Set a timer for 1 hour and take a break. By the time you come back the dough should be beautifully puffy and doubled in size. If not, set a timer for 30 minutes and check again. Punch the dough down. If you want to start this the night before, stop here, reseal the plastic, and refrigerate overnight. Leave out at room temperature for 30 minutes before rolling.

Lightly spritz the counter with nonstick spray and lay down a piece of parchment paper that's at least 12 by 16-inches, pressing to stick on the spray. Lightly

*Inngredients and recipe continue*

**GLAZE**

3 cups (360 grams) powdered
  sugar
2 tablespoons cocoa powder
1 teaspoon peppermint extract
  (optional)
2 tablespoons pure maple syrup
1 teaspoon ground cardamom
  (optional)
Red food coloring
1 teaspoon pure vanilla extract
3 tablespoons whole milk, plus
  more as needed
Rainbow sprinkles

**SPECIAL EQUIPMENT**

Stand mixer
3-inch and 1-inch cutters
Candy or deep-fry thermometer

spray the top of the parchment, too. Turn the dough onto the parchment and pat into a rough square. Use a rolling pin to gently roll out from the center to make a 10 by 14-inch rectangle. If the parchment is too slick to roll, lift the dough and sprinkle a little flour underneath. It doesn't have to be a flawless rectangle with perfect lines, but try to roll the dough to an even thickness.

Use a 3-inch cutter to lightly pre-mark 13 donuts spread out across the dough. Go back and press the cutter down on each mark, twisting a little for a clean cut. If the dough is sticky, scoop some flour on a small plate and twirl the cutter in it before each cut. Go back through with the 1-inch cutter to cut out 13 holes from the center of each donut. Peel all the dough scraps away and discard (see Party Tricks). Lift the holes out of the donuts and set them in empty spaces around the parchment. Lightly drape plastic over all of the cutouts and set a timer for 15 minutes to let the dough relax and puff slightly.

**While the dough is resting, make the glaze:** Line up three small bowls. Tap 1 cup (120 grams) of powdered sugar into each bowl. In the first bowl, add the cocoa powder and peppermint extract, if you're using it. In the second bowl, add the maple syrup and cardamom, if you have it. In the last bowl, add 1 drop of red food coloring and the vanilla. Add 1 tablespoon of milk to each bowl. Whisk the chocolate bowl to make a smooth, slightly thick icing. It should very slowly drizzle off the whisk. Add 1 teaspoon of milk if it needs it. Rinse and dry the whisk, then repeat for the maple bowl, then the vanilla bowl. The vanilla icing should be a pale pink, so add another drop of red if it needs it.

When the timer goes off, pour the vegetable oil into a large Dutch oven and clip the thermometer to the side. Set over medium heat to start warming up and keep a careful eye on the thermometer. Set a wire rack over a rimmed baking sheet and keep it near the Dutch oven. As soon as the thermometer hits 375°F, carefully lower three of the donuts and a few of the holes into the oil. Fry for about 2 minutes, then use a spider strainer or slotted spoon to flip and fry for about 2 more minutes. You don't need a timer, just watch the dough turn a very donut-like shade of golden brown. Transfer the donuts to the wire rack to drain. Let the oil come up to 375°F again, then add the next batch of donuts and holes. Repeat again, then finish with a final batch of four. Remove the Dutch oven from the stove and cover (see Party Tricks).

Whisk the glazes again. While the donuts are still hot, dip one side in one of the glazes and set it on the wire rack to dry. Give the pink donuts (or all the donuts) a pinch of rainbow sprinkles before the glaze sets. Use a spoon to roll the donut holes in the glazes to completely coat before setting on the wire rack. The donuts can be served or packed up as soon as the glaze sets. They should be eaten within a few hours of frying, which never seems to be a problem.

## PARTY TRICKS

- To be sure you're ready to rise, do a windowpane test. Rip off a Ping-Pong-ball-size amount of dough and slowly stretch it between your hands until it's thin enough for light to pass through. If the dough rips, put it back in the mixer on medium speed and set a timer for another 5 minutes before testing again.

- Technically, you could reroll the dough scraps, but I wouldn't recommend it. The dough will just get stickier, overworked, and tough. Scrap dough does comes in handy if you don't have a thermometer—use a piece to check your oil temp.

- Let the oil cool completely, covered and away from the stove for safety's sake, over a few hours. Strain it into a large measuring cup and pour it into the container it came in. If the oil is still in decent shape, store it in the refrigerator and use it the next time you fry. (As long as that time is in the next 2 weeks.) If it's nasty, throw it out. Never pour oil down the drain or in the toilet—it'll murder your pipes.

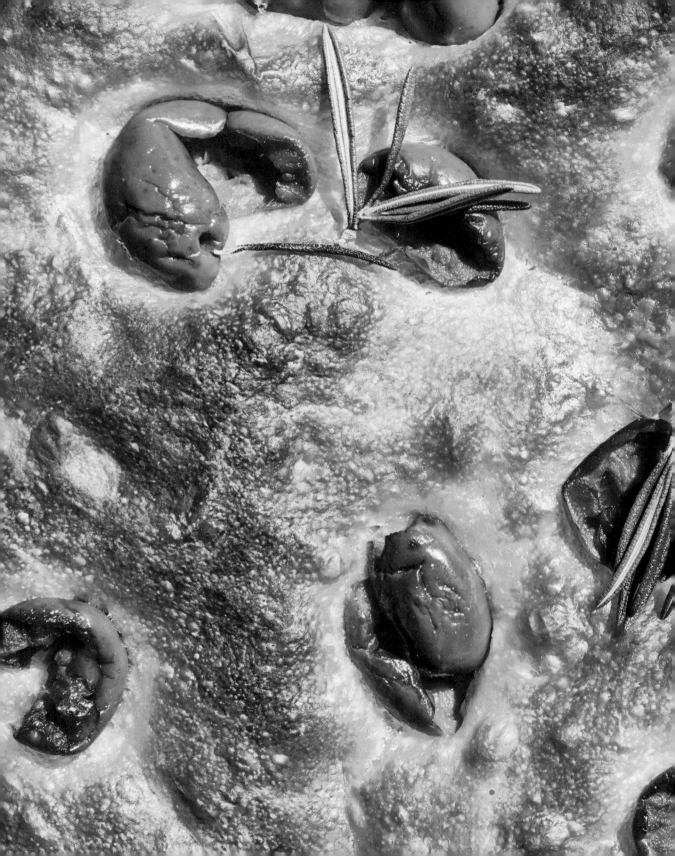

ON THE
RISE

**I CAN'T THINK** of a dinner, picnic, or snack board that isn't immediately improved with really great bread. In this chapter, you'll find plenty of soft-and-fluffy, bubbly-and-crusty, and dense-and-savory options that are actually enjoyable to make and execute, even if you're still getting comfortable with your oven. And for the real overachievers and proud show-offs, come on in! There are plenty of big projects here for you, too.

# Cornmeal Crackers

IN YOUR SLEEP | VG, NF (GF)

I grew up on a steady diet of **Martha Stewart's** books and shows, so it's natural that when I'm lost and need inspiration, I turn to my patron saint and ask myself, *What would Martha do?* I think these cornmeal crackers are exactly what Martha would do. Yes, of course you could just go out and buy a nice box of artisanal crackers, but there is nothing more simultaneously passive-aggressive and effortlessly chic than rolling in with a batch of homemade crackers. The cornmeal has a very pleasing texture, the cheddar gives just a hint of Cheez-It, and a spicy pinch of chile gives it a pleasing little kick. It's—and I'm speaking for myself *and* Martha here—a good thing.

*(Pictured on page 26)*

**Makes 32 crackers**

1 cup (160 grams) cornmeal

1 cup (140 grams) all-purpose flour or gluten-free flour, plus more as needed (see Party Tricks on page 215)

¼ cup (30 grams) grated extra-sharp white or orange cheddar cheese

2 tablespoons unsalted butter, at room temperature

2 teaspoons kosher salt

2 teaspoons sugar

½ teaspoon red pepper flakes or other chile flakes (see Party Trick on page 223 for my favorites)

In a food processor, combine the cornmeal, flour, cheddar, butter, salt, sugar, red pepper flakes, and ¾ cup of warm water. Run the processor until a ball forms, about 1 minute. If it's sticky, mix in more flour, 1 tablespoon at a time, and process. When you have a cohesive, hydrated ball of dough, turn it out onto the counter. Divide into two equal portions, pat into fat discs, wrap tightly in plastic wrap, and set a timer for 30 minutes to rest.

Preheat the oven to 400°F and set a rack in the center.

Set one of the discs between two pieces of parchment and roll it into a 9 by 13-inch rectangle. Remove the top parchment but keep it handy. Trim ½ inch off each side of the dough to make a perfectly straight 8 by 12-inch rectangle. (I like to use a ruler and pizza cutter to make this a breeze, but a chef's knife works, too!) On the 8-inch edges, measure and nick a mark every 2 inches. On the 12-inch edges, measure and nick a mark 3 inches. Cut across from one nick to the other to make 16 equal pieces. Lift the parchment onto a rimmed baking sheet and evenly space out the squares. Press the tip of a fork's tines in the center of each cracker to dock little holes.

Slide the baking sheet into the oven and set a timer for 15 minutes. The crackers should be golden and crisp. If not, set a timer for 5 minutes and test again. Set aside to cool completely on the baking sheet, about 1 hour. While the first batch bakes, roll, trim, and cut the second ball of dough. (Use the reserved parchment as the top piece again!) Slide the parchment onto a second rimmed baking sheet before separating, docking, baking, and cooling.

## PARTY TRICK

- Leftover crackers can be stored in a zip-top bag at room temperature for up to 1 week.

# Herby Challah

ROLL UP YOUR SLEEVES | VG, NF

*Optional: Start this recipe 1 day ahead.*

Challah is a staple of Shabbat and the Jewish holidays. For me, a goy, it's a staple all the time because it is simply a perfect loaf of bread. The richness of the eggs and shortening, the slight sweetness, the gorgeous braid, the deep brown color are all the things of my carb dreams. I like to incorporate a bouquet of herbs inside and a vibrant green sprinkle of scallions on top for a nice savory touch to a lunch or dinner. If you want to hang a little sweeter or a little more classic, leave all the herbs out and it's still a great loaf of challah.

## Makes 1 large loaf

1 (0.25-ounce) packet instant yeast (see Party Trick on page 104)
¼ cup shortening (50 grams), such as Crisco, melted
¼ cup (75 grams) honey
3⅓ cups (465 grams) all-purpose flour, plus more for dusting
2 cups packed mixed herbs, such as thyme, rosemary, tarragon, parsley, chives, dill, cilantro, or oregano, finely chopped
3 large egg yolks
2½ teaspoons kosher salt
Nonstick cooking spray
3 scallions, cut into ½-inch pieces
2 teaspoons vegetable oil
Flaky salt, freshly ground black pepper, and/or red pepper flakes (optional)

### SPECIAL EQUIPMENT
Stand mixer

In the bowl of a stand mixer fitted with the dough hook, combine the yeast and 1 cup (230 grams) warm tap water. Swirl the melted shortening in the ¼ cup measure and pour it into the bowl, then measure the honey so it slides right out of the cup. Add the flour, herbs, and 2 of the egg yolks. Cover and refrigerate that third yolk for later!

Start mixing on low speed until the dough comes together, about 3 minutes. Sprinkle in the salt and turn the speed up to medium. Set a timer for 10 minutes, until the dough is smooth, a little sticky, and the bowl is mostly clean. Coat a large bowl with nonstick spray and scrape the dough in. Cover tightly with plastic wrap and set somewhere warm to rise (see Party Tricks on page 104 for a great idea) and set a timer for 1 hour. The dough should be roughly doubled in size, but if not give it another 30 minutes. (If you want to make this a two-day project, skip this rise and refrigerate the dough for at least 12 hours or up to 24 hours.)

Lightly flour one side of the counter. Line a rimmed baking sheet with parchment paper. Punch the dough down and scrape it out onto the floured side of the counter. Pat the dough into a rough square and cut it into three equal pieces. Working one piece at a time, move over to the unfloured side of the counter. Fold the far edge of the dough into the center and use your fingers to seal the seam. Fold the near edge into the center and seal again. Now use one hand to fold the far edge over to touch the near edge and use the fingers of your other hand to press the seam shut, gradually working your way down the length of the dough. Repeat with the other two pieces, then cover with a damp kitchen towel and set a timer for 10 minutes to let the gluten relax.

Set one hand in the center of a dough piece and roll it into a dog bone shape. Set both hands in the center and firmly roll outward into an 18-inch-long rope. As

*Recipe continues*

you get toward the end, roll rapidly in opposite directions to taper the ends. As you roll each dough piece, lay the ropes diagonally across the prepared baking sheet. Start in the center of the ropes and drape the pieces over each other to start a braid. Braid outward to one end of the dough—gently draping, not pulling—until you can pinch the tips together. Press down with your thumb to seal the end, then tuck it under. Finish the braid outward in the other direction, then seal and tuck the tip under. Cover the baking sheet with a damp kitchen towel and set it somewhere warm (but not the oven). Set a timer for 60 minutes, and if the loaf isn't doubled by then, give it 30 more.

While the dough is resting, preheat the oven to 325°F and set a rack in the center.

Add 1 tablespoon of cold water to the egg yolk we saved and whisk it well. Just before baking, brush the entire loaf, including the sides, with a thin layer of egg wash. In a small bowl, toss the scallions and vegetable oil to coat. Evenly sprinkle the scallions in the creases along the top of the braid. Sprinkle the surface of the dough with flaky salt and a few good cracks of pepper. (Or a pinch of red pepper flakes for a spicy touch.)

Slide the baking sheet into the oven and set a timer for 15 minutes. (Keep that door shut!) When the timer goes off, increase the oven temp to 400°F and set a timer for 15 more minutes. The loaf should be deeply browned—I like to go an extra 5 minutes for extra browning, but every oven is different—and sound hollow when tapped on the bottom. Cool completely on the baking sheet, about 2 hours, before slicing.

### PARTY TRICK

- Leftover bread can be stored in a zip-top bag at room temperature for up to 3 days.

# Potato Parker House Rolls

ROLL UP YOUR SLEEVES | VG, NF

If there are warm dinner rolls nearby, get out of my way. This recipe makes a generous amount of rolls because they are guaranteed to fly. Potato flakes, one of my favorite secret weapons, add a soft, starchy texture without the hassle of cooking, mashing, and cooling actual potatoes. With the bonus of an easy Japanese technique called yudane (more on that below) and butter that's both slowly mixed in and twice brushed all over the top, these are the dream version of a soft, buttery, pull-apart dinner roll.

## Makes 24 rolls

Nonstick cooking spray
3 cups (420 grams) all-purpose flour
1 cup (100 grams) potato flakes, plain or butter flavor
1 (0.25-ounce) packet instant yeast (see Party Trick on page 104)
¼ cup (50 grams) sugar
1 cup (230 grams) whole milk
1 large egg
1½ teaspoons kosher salt
½ cup (1 stick) unsalted butter, at room temperature
Nonstick cooking spray
Flaky sea salt, for garnish

### SPECIAL EQUIPMENT
Stand mixer

Set a large saucepan of water to boil over high heat. When the water is at a ripping boil, pour a little into the bowl of a stand mixer and swirl to warm up the inside of the bowl. Dump that water out, then pour in ⅓ cup (70 grams) of the boiling water. Add ½ cup (70 grams) of the flour and use a rubber spatula to stir the water and flour together to make a soft dough. (See Party Tricks.)

Attach the bowl to the stand mixer and fit the mixer with the dough hook. Add the remaining 2½ cups (350 grams) flour with the potato flakes, yeast, sugar, milk, and egg. Mix on low until the dough starts coming together. With the mixer running, add the salt. Use a butter knife to cut the butter stick in half. Set half of it aside for later. Cut off 1 tablespoon of butter at a time, tapping it into the bowl and letting it fully mix in before adding another, that's 4 tablespoons total. Once all the fat is mixed in, increase the speed to medium and set a timer for 8 minutes. The dough will start out wet and sticky, but eventually it'll hydrate and pull together. (Add an additional 1 tablespoon water at this stage if the dough needs it.) When the timer goes off, it should be smooth, barely sticky, and the sides of the bowl should be clean.

Coat a large bowl with nonstick spray and scrape in the dough. Cover tightly with plastic wrap and set somewhere warm to rise (see Party Tricks on page 104 for a cozy place). Set a timer for 60 minutes and check on the dough. It'll be puffy and maybe just starting to rise, but not doubled in size. If it still seems about the same, give it another 30 minutes.

Coat a 9 by 13-inch baking pan with nonstick spray. Turn the dough out onto the counter and pat it into a rough square. Use a sharp knife to cut the dough into 24 same-ish sized pieces and roll each one into roughly 2-inch balls. Arrange the dough balls in 6 rows of 4 in the baking pan, about ½ inch apart. Cover the top of the pan with plastic wrap and set somewhere warm to rise. (But not the oven this time!) Set a timer for 60 minutes. If the rolls aren't touching yet, give them another 15 to 30 minutes.

*Recipe continues*

Before the rolls are done rising, preheat the oven to 350°F and set a rack in the center.

In a small saucepan, melt the remaining 4 tablespoons butter over low heat. When the rolls are ready, discard the plastic and brush the tops of the dough with about half of the butter and generously sprinkle with flaky salt. Slide the pan in the oven and set a timer for 25 minutes. The rolls should be puffy, golden brown, and feel set if you lightly press down on one. If not, give them 5 more minutes. While they're hot out of the oven, gently dab the rolls with the rest of the butter. Let cool for at least 30 minutes before serving, or cool completely in the pan, about 2 hours.

## PARTY TRICKS

- This method is called yudane, a Japanese technique for gelatinizing the starch in flour. It'll make the rolls more tender and springy, and will preserve the softness for a surprisingly long time.

- Cover the top of the pan with aluminum foil if you're traveling with it. The rolls can be served at room temperature or rewarmed in a 300°F oven for 10 minutes.

- Leftover bread can be stored in a zip-top bag at room temperature for up to 5 days.

# Cheese Twists

IN YOUR SLEEP | VG, NF (GF)

This is Part One in a two-part series we'll call Repurposing Freezer Dough: Breads for Those a Little Nervous to Bake. (Part Two is Scrunchy Bread on page 140.) You know who has never let anyone down? Store-bought puff pastry. It's tender, flaky, doughy, and just so perfect as a cute little cheesy twist. These are perfect dates to a cocktail party or fun little companions alongside a cheese board, and the easiest compliment magnets you'll ever make.

**Makes 12 twists**

2 sheets frozen puff pastry (from a 17.3-ounce box), thawed, gluten-free if you want

2 tablespoons heavy cream

1 cup (100 grams) plus 3 tablespoons grated pecorino cheese (see Party Tricks)

3 tablespoons fresh thyme leaves

1 teaspoon garlic powder

2 tablespoons sesame seeds

¼ teaspoon kosher salt

**Remember to set the puff pastry in the refrigerator overnight to thaw.**

Preheat the oven to 400°F and set a rack in the center. Line two rimmed baking sheets with parchment paper.

Lay another piece of parchment on the counter and unfold a puff pastry sheet in the center. Brush 1 tablespoon of the cream evenly over the entire surface. In a small bowl, pinch together 1 cup of the pecorino plus the thyme leaves and garlic powder, then sprinkle the mixture evenly over the pastry. Unfold the other pastry sheet on top and pinch the edges together to seal.

Use a rolling pin to roll into a 12 by 14-inch rectangle. Brush the remaining 1 tablespoon cream on top. In the same bowl, pinch the remaining 3 tablespoons pecorino, the sesame seeds, and salt together, then sprinkle them over the entire surface. On the 12-inch edges, measure and nick a mark every inch. Cut across from one nick to the other to make twelve 14-inch-long strips. Working one strip at a time, bend it into a U shape, then twist the ends around each other three times and pinch the final twist to seal. Arrange 6 of the twists evenly spaced on one of the baking sheets, then slide it into the oven and set a timer for 15 minutes. While those twists are baking, shape and arrange the remaining strips on the other baking sheet.

When the timer goes off, check the twists. They should be puffed and beautifully golden. (Give them 2 more minutes if they need it.) Move the twists to a wire rack to cool and bake the other sheet. Let cool completely, about 30 minutes.

## PARTY TRICKS

- If you want an extra special touch, there is really nothing better than freshly grated Locatelli cheese.

- These are perfect room temperature and don't reheat all that well anyway!

- Any leftover bread can be stored in a zip-top bag at room temperature for up to 2 days.

# Blender Cornbread

IN YOUR SLEEP | VG, NF (GF)

A quick whirl in the blender, straight into the pan, and that's it. This is the foolproof bread if ever there was one, but we're making *zero* compromises on flavor. Adding a cup of frozen corn to the batter is all it takes to make this the absolute top tier most flavorful cornbread you, me, and everyone we know has ever had. When you really want to bring something homemade, but bread has always felt scary, this is the one for you.

**Makes an 8-inch round**

Nonstick cooking spray
2 tablespoons plus 1 cup (160 grams) cornmeal
1 cup (230 grams) whole milk
½ cup (1 stick) unsalted butter, melted
½ cup (100 grams) sugar
2 tablespoons vegetable oil
1 cup (140 grams) frozen corn, thawed
2 teaspoons baking powder
1 teaspoon kosher salt
½ cup (70 grams) all-purpose flour or gluten-free flour (see Party Trick on page 215)

Preheat the oven to 350°F and set a rack in the center. Set an 8-inch (or 9-inch) cake pan right-side up on a piece of parchment. Trace around the bottom of the pan, then cut around the inside of the circle to avoid the ink. Coat the bottom and sides of the pan with nonstick spray, press the parchment round to the bottom, and spray again. Sprinkle 2 tablespoons of cornmeal in the pan, then hold it over the sink to tap and spread the cornmeal all over the bottom and sides of the pan.

In the blender, layer the ingredients in exactly this order: milk at the bottom, then the butter, sugar, vegetable oil, corn, baking powder, salt, flour, and, finally, the remaining 1 cup cornmeal. Put the lid on and start the blender at low speed and work up to high, just until you have a smooth batter. Pour it into the prepared pan, tapping on the blender or using a rubber spatula to scrape it all out. Wiggle the cake pan to even it out.

Slide the pan into the oven and set a timer for 45 minutes. (If you're using a 9-inch cake pan, set the timer for 40 minutes.) Slide a toothpick into the center of the cornbread. If it comes out clean or with a few crumbs, you're good. If not, set a timer for 5 minutes and test again. Set aside to cool completely in the pan, about 1 hour.

## PARTY TRICKS

- Cover the top of the pan with aluminum foil if you're traveling with it. It can be served at room temperature or rewarmed in a 300°F oven for 10 minutes. I think it looks very cute served straight out of the cake pan.

- Leftover cornbread can be stored in a zip-top bag at room temperature for up to 3 days.

# Fluffy Pitas

ROLL UP YOUR SLEEVES | V, NF

*Start this recipe 1 day ahead.*

These are the taffeta ball gowns of pitas. What I mean is this is no time for pockets. We're going for thick and fluffy as hell. They are genetically engineered to be set out next to any dip and torn apart by hungry hands. They're also engineered to go straight from the fridge into the oven so you can make these moments before you walk out the door and arrive with them piping hot. I'll admit I very frequently make these for myself at home, too, because practice makes perfect!

**Makes 8 pitas**

2¾ cups (385 grams)
  unbleached bread flour (see
  Party Tricks)
1 (0.25-ounce) packet instant
  yeast (see Party Trick on
  page 104)
1 tablespoon honey or sugar
1 tablespoon extra-virgin olive
  oil, plus more for the bowl
2 teaspoons kosher salt

**SPECIAL EQUIPMENT**
Stand mixer

In the bowl of a stand mixer, whisk together ¾ cup (105 grams) of the flour, the yeast, honey, and 1 cup (230 grams) warm tap water. Fit the dough hook to the mixer and add the olive oil and another 1 cup (140 grams) of the flour to the mixer bowl. Mix on low speed until a sticky dough forms, about 2 minutes. Scrape down the sides, then add the salt and the remaining 1 cup (140 grams) flour. Start mixing on low to get the flour incorporated, then increase the speed to high and set a timer for 5 minutes. The dough should be smooth, a little sticky, and the sides of the bowl should be clean.

Lift the dough up, drizzle a little olive oil in the bowl, and plop the dough back in. Cover the bowl tightly with plastic wrap and put it in a warm place to rise. (See Party Tricks on page 104 for a secret spot.) Set a timer for 1 hour and take a break. By the time you come back the dough should be beautifully puffy and doubled in size. If not, set a timer for 30 minutes and check again.

Lightly dust half the counter with flour. Punch the dough down and scrape it out onto the floured side of the counter. Pat it into a rough rectangle and use a knife or a bench scraper to cut the dough into 8 equal pieces. With each piece, create a smooth ball by tucking the edges under. Set the ball on the unfloured side of the counter, seam side down, and lightly cup your hand over it with your thumb and pinkie firmly on the counter. Roll, using the heel of your hand, thumb, and pinkie as barriers against the ball, then place the ball back on the floured side. Keep rolling and space the balls about 2 inches apart on the counter. Sprinkle a little more flour on top of the balls and cover loosely with plastic wrap. Set a timer for 30 minutes.

Preheat the oven to 500°F and set a rack in the lowest position. Set an upside-down baking sheet or a baking stone on the rack to preheat.

*Recipe continues*

Lightly dust the other side of the counter with more flour. Working one at a time, remove a ball and use you palm to press it flat into a small circle. (Keep the other balls covered until it's their turn.) Grab a rolling pin or wine bottle and roll into a rough and imperfect 5-inch circle, dusting with more flour to prevent any sticking. Roll out 2 of the balls, then set a timer for 10 minutes to let them air dry. Roll out 2 more balls while those are resting and let them start drying.

When the timer goes off, roll out the last 4 balls and let them dry out. Slide the low rack out and lift the first two circles on the preheated sheet. Immediately shut the oven and set a timer for 2 minutes. Use a wide spatula to flip the pitas and bake for 2 more minutes just so the bottoms can brown. Immediately remove and wrap in a thick kitchen towel to keep warm. Continue baking the rest of the pitas in the order that you rolled them.

### PARTY TRICKS

- This can be done with all-purpose flour, but you'll get a much better rise and texture with a higher-protein bread flour.

- Once all the pitas are cozy in their towel, slip the entire towel into a zip-top bag and seal to keep the pitas warm and soft if you'll be serving them soon. Otherwise, they can be wrapped in aluminum foil and reheated in a 300°F oven for 10 minutes or flipped over a gas burner for a couple seconds on each side to warm up.

- Any leftover pitas can be stored in a zip-top bag at room temperature for up to 2 days.

# Seeded Barbari

ROLL UP YOUR SLEEVES | V, NF

This Persian flatbread (full name: nan-e barbari) is pillowy, chewy, and literally heaven. It's traditionally paired with a briny feta-like cheese called Lighvan, and maybe some tender herbs and sliced cucumbers for a fresh bite, which just lets you know this bread is perfect for a snack board, alongside a salad, or torn into pieces and dragged through a creamy dip. Usually a trio of seeds—sesame, nigella, and poppy—get sprinkled over the dough before baking, but I like to also mix them inside the bread so every bite has surprising layers of flavor and texture. The best part is an ingenious glaze of flour, baking soda, and oil that acts almost like an eggless egg wash, giving the top of the loaf a perfect golden sheen.

**Makes 2 big flatbreads**

### DOUGH

3½ cups (490 grams) unbleached bread flour (see Party Tricks on page 136)
1 (0.25-ounce) packet instant yeast (see Party Tricks on page 104)
1 tablespoon white or black sesame seeds
1 tablespoon nigella seeds (see Party Tricks)
1 tablespoon poppy seeds
1 teaspoon sugar
2 teaspoons kosher salt
Nonstick cooking spray

### TOPPING

2 teaspoons unbleached bread flour or all-purpose flour
1 teaspoon extra-virgin olive oil
1 teaspoon baking soda
1 tablespoon white or black sesame seeds
1 tablespoon nigella seeds
1 tablespoon poppy seeds
Flaky sea salt

**Make the dough:** In the bowl of a stand mixer fitted with the dough hook, combine the flour, yeast, sesame seeds, nigella seeds, poppy seeds, sugar, and 1½ cups (340 grams) of warm tap water. Mix on low until a sticky dough forms, about 2 minutes. Add the salt and increase the speed to high and set a timer for 8 minutes. The dough should be smooth, a little sticky, and the sides of the bowl should be clean. Coat a large bowl with nonstick spray and scrape the dough in. Cover tightly with plastic wrap and set somewhere warm to rise (see Party Tricks on page 104 for the perfect place) and set a timer for 1 hour. The dough should double (a little more or less is fine) in size and it can have another 30 minutes if it needs it.

Keep a small bowl of warm water nearby and lay two sheets of parchment on the counter. Dip a hand in the water and punch the dough down and divide it in half. Transfer each half to a piece of parchment and, dipping your fingers as needed, press into a roughly 12 by 6-inch rectangle with tapered ends. Lightly coat a piece of plastic wrap with nonstick spray and lay it over each rectangle of dough. Set a timer for 30 minutes, just to let the dough relax and puff a little.

As soon as the dough is resting, preheat the oven to 500°F and set a rack in the lowest position. Set an upside-down baking sheet or a baking stone on the rack to preheat.

**Make the topping:** In a small saucepan, combine the flour, olive oil, baking soda, and 3 tablespoons water. Set over medium heat and use a rubber spatula to stir constantly until the mixture thickens and coats the spatula, about 2 minutes. Remove from the heat to cool.

*Recipe continues*

White Beans +
Tinned Fish, 33

Fried Halloumi
Caprese, 78

When the dough is ready, wet your fingertips again. Press four long grooves across the length of one dough rectangle. Brush the top with half of the flour mixture, then sprinkle half of the seeds on top followed by a couple good pinches of flaky salt. Open the oven and slide the bottom rack out. Use the parchment to airlift the loaf onto the baking sheet. Quickly shut the oven and set a timer for 15 minutes. The loaf should be nicely golden brown and just a little puffy, but give it 5 more minutes if it's looking a little pale. Use tongs to move the loaf to a wire rack to cool and discard the parchment. While the first loaf bakes, press, brush, and sprinkle the second loaf, then bake. Cool the loaves for at least 15 minutes before serving.

## PARTY TRICKS

- If you can't find nigella seeds, just add more sesame, poppy, or a little of both. A tablespoon each of garlic and onion flakes in the dough pushes this in a very nontraditional but satisfying everything bagel direction.

- The loaves can be served at room temperature or wrapped in foil and rewarmed in a 300°F oven for 10 minutes.

- Any leftover bread can be stored in a zip-top bag at room temperature for up to 3 days.

# Scrunchy Bread

IN YOUR SLEEP | VG, NF

Welcome to Part Two of freezer dough reinvented. (For Part One, see Cheese Twists on page 130). Phyllo is our focus this time for a round loaf that's all crispy, shattering layers on the outside, all warm and savory on the inside. Blending up sun-dried tomatoes with feta will get you a perfectly salty, rich center and then it's just dabbing a little olive oil as you layer up the phyllo and filling. This is the "Wow, what is in this?" moment we all fantasize about.

**Makes an 8-inch round**

1 (16-ounce) box frozen phyllo dough, thawed
1 (8-ounce) jar sun-dried tomatoes in oil
6 ounces feta
2 tablespoons fresh oregano leaves
1½ cups extra-virgin olive oil
Sesame seeds and freshly ground black pepper

**Remember to set the phyllo dough in the refrigerator overnight to thaw.**

Preheat the oven to 375°F and set a rack in the center. Dip a pastry brush into the sun-dried tomato oil and lightly brush the bottom and sides of an 8-inch (or 9-inch) cake pan. Fold a piece of parchment in half lengthwise and press to adhere across the cake pan (for an easy lift later) and brush that too.

In a blender or food processor, combine the sun-dried tomatoes with the rest of their oil, the feta broken into rough crumbles, and oregano. Process until a smooth mixture forms. Reserve 2 tablespoons in a small bowl and keep the rest in the blender.

Unroll the phyllo on a clean counter. Pour 1 cup of the olive oil into a small bowl. Lay a sheet of phyllo in the pan, letting the edges hang over. Dip a pastry brush in the olive oil and lightly brush the dough. Repeat this until you have 10 layers of dough on the bottom. Don't worry if any of the sheets tear, it's all baking together anyway. Pour about half of the tomato mixture over the phyllo and use a spatula to spread in an even layer. Continue layering and brushing the rest of the sheets, then pour the rest of the tomato mixture and spread again.

Whisk the reserved tomato mixture with the remaining ½ cup olive oil. Start folding the overhang into the center a couple pieces at a time and lightly brushing the top with the tomato oil. I like to spread the first few pieces flat so the filling is covered, then start making pretty scrunches around the surface with the rest. (You can even trim off some of the overhang to twist and scrunch and place around the top.) Brush any remaining tomato oil over the top, then generously sprinkle sesame seeds and some good cracks of pepper across the surface.

Slide the pan into the oven and set a timer for 45 minutes. The phyllo should be golden brown and crispy, but give it another 5 minutes if you think it needs it. Cool for 15 minutes (or completely) in the pan, then use the parchment to airlift it to a cutting board or serving plate. Slide the parchment out from underneath before slicing and serving.

## PARTY TRICKS

- This is perfect at room temperature, but if you really want to serve it hot, assemble everything at home and cover the top of the pan before transporting. Plan your oven space ahead of time with your host, bake it, cool for 15 minutes in the pan, then use the parchment to lift out and serve right away.

- Any leftover bread can be stored in a zip-top bag at room temperature for up to 2 days.

Olive +
Rosemary

Grape +
Balsamic

Prosciutto +
Parm

# Dreamy Focaccia

ROLL UP YOUR SLEEVES | V, NF

*Optional: Start this recipe 1 day ahead.*

I would rank focaccia at the tippity top of my carby pleasures. A good loaf should be loaded with bubbles, a little crunchy outside, springy soft inside, so absolutely drenched in oil, and topped with just the right things. (I have three ideas for the right things on page 144, just to get your gears turning.) Even though we passed the brunch chapter already, my little secret is I like to make this the day before and bring it the next morning—it's like the adult version of pizza for breakfast. But focaccia is the right move all day, especially when it's still a little warm or cut into small slices and stacked next to the cheese board at a dinner party.

**Makes one sheet pan focaccia**

2 cups (455 grams) warm tap water
1 (0.25-ounce) packet instant yeast (see Party Tricks on page 104)
2 tablespoons extra-virgin olive oil, plus a lot more for the pan
2 tablespoons honey or 1 tablespoon sugar
4 cups (560 grams) unbleached bread flour
1 tablespoon kosher salt
Toppings (see chart below)

In a large bowl, lightly whisk the water and yeast. Add the olive oil and honey (in alternating tablespoons so the honey slides out), then the flour and salt and use a wooden spoon to stir into a wet and sticky dough. When all the flour is hydrated, use a rubber spatula to scrape down the sides of the bowl and cover tightly with plastic wrap. Set a timer for 30 minutes.

Keep a small bowl of warm water nearby. Remove the plastic but keep it nearby. Dip your hand in the water. Reach across the bowl and slide your hand under the dough. Lift it up and bring it across the bowl and drop it in front of you. Rotate the bowl a quarter turn, dip your hand in the water, reach across, then lift and drop the dough. Do this rotation two more times until you've folded all four sides. Cover the bowl with the plastic and set a timer for 30 minutes. You're going to repeat this folding and resting process three more times, which will take 2 hours of your time but only a few minutes of actual work. (This is a good time to watch a movie or clean your house.) The dough should get progressively bubblier and easier to work with as you go. After the fourth and final round of folding, cover the dough again. You can either continue with the recipe right now or refrigerate the dough overnight.

Whether the dough is freshly out of the folding or fresh out of the refrigerator, the next step is the same: Set a timer for 30 minutes. (Ugh, last time, I promise!) While you're waiting, line a rimmed baking sheet with parchment paper and generously drizzle olive oil all over the place. Like very generously, almost ½ cup. When the timer goes off, discard the plastic. Rub your hands over the baking sheet to spread the oil. Swirl your greasy hands around the dough to gather it into a rough ball, almost like a fold rotation but not as formal.

*Recipe continues*

Immediately lift the dough onto the baking sheet, then gently lift and wiggle the ends to encourage the dough to stretch out. When the dough is covering about 75 percent of the baking sheet, flip a second baking sheet on top as a cover. Set a timer for 60 minutes. (I'm so sorry I lied before, I thought you were going to leave me. This is for real the final rest.)

While the dough rests, preheat the oven to 450°F and set racks in the upper and lower third.

When the timer goes off, the focaccia should be puffy and taking up space. Drizzle olive oil all over the top of the dough and a little on your hands. If it needs coaxing to fill out the pan, lift the edges and wiggle a little to stretch it out. Then use your fingers to dimple all over the dough, wiggling your hands to help evenly spread the dough across the sheet. Add any toppings you want, then slide the baking sheet on the low rack and set a timer for 15 minutes. Move it to the upper rack and set a timer for 10 minutes. The focaccia should be gorgeous and golden brown all over. Give it another 5 minutes if it needs it. Cool on the sheet for 10 minutes, then slide it onto a wire rack. Cool for at least 15 more minutes before slicing, or cool completely. Any leftover bread can be stored in a zip-top bag at room temperature for up to 2 days.

| TOPPINGS | |
| --- | --- |
| **OLIVE + ROSEMARY** | Toss ½ cup pitted Castelvetrano olives with 1 tablespoon extra-virgin olive oil, then scatter them in the dimples. While the focaccia bakes, slide your fingers down 3 or 4 rosemary stems to remove the leaves in little bundles. As soon as the focaccia comes out of the oven, sprinkle the rosemary on top along with a couple pinches of red pepper flakes. Some freshly grated orange zest wouldn't hurt either. |
| **GRAPE + BALSAMIC** | Toss ½ cup seedless red or Concord grapes plus 1 tablespoon fennel seeds with 1 tablespoon extra-virgin olive oil, then scatter them in the dimples. As soon as the focaccia comes out of the oven, drizzle balsamic glaze over the top and finish with a couple pinches of flaky sea salt. |
| **PROSCIUTTO + PARM** | Drape and fold 3 ounces of thinly sliced prosciutto over the dough. Toss ½ thinly sliced red onion with 1 tablespoon extra-virgin olive oil and sprinkle it over the prosciutto. As soon as the focaccia comes out of the oven, use a rasp grater to blanket the top with fresh Parmesan and finish with a few good cracks of black pepper. |

# Parmesan Round

ROLL UP YOUR SLEEVES | VG, NF (GF)

This is a big and spongy round that's going to be an instant hit at any dinner party. I'm sidestepping the word *bread* because we really have to give the whipped egg whites all the credit here. They do the hard work, giving lots of height and air, and the small amount of flour really just holds it all together. If the time commitment of a focaccia (page 143) just isn't in the cards for you, this has a similar vibe and will hit the same satisfying spot.

**Makes an 8-inch round**

Nonstick cooking spray

**BREAD**
1 cup (140 grams) all-purpose flour or gluten-free flour (see Party Tricks on page 215)
½ cup (80 grams) cornmeal
2 teaspoons baking powder
1 teaspoon kosher salt
½ teaspoon freshly ground black pepper
3 large eggs
½ cup (115 grams) whole milk
6 tablespoons unsalted butter, melted
¾ cup (75 grams) freshly grated Parmesan cheese
½ teaspoon cream of tartar

**TOPPING**
2 garlic cloves, thinly sliced
2 tablespoons fresh rosemary leaves
1 tablespoon extra-virgin olive oil
¼ teaspoon red pepper flakes

Preheat the oven to 375°F and set a rack in the center. Set an 8-inch (or 9-inch) cake pan right-side up on a piece of parchment paper. Trace around the bottom of the pan, then cut around the inside of the circle to avoid the ink. Coat the bottom and sides of the pan with nonstick spray, press the parchment round to the bottom, and spray again.

**Make the bread:** Set a large bowl and medium bowl next to each other. In the large bowl, whisk the flour, cornmeal, baking powder, salt, and pepper together. Make a little well in the middle of the flour. Crack the eggs, letting the whites drop into the empty medium bowl and plopping the yolks in the large bowl's flour well. Set the whites aside for a second. Whisk the yolks just to break them up, then whisk the milk, butter, and Parmesan into the well. Switch to a spatula to fold the wet and dry ingredients together.

Going back to the whites, add the cream of tartar to the bowl. Wash and dry your whisk, then beat the whites until they're puffy and soft, about 5 minutes. When you lift the whisk out of the whites and flip it up, it should make a peak that droops to the side. Use the spatula to scoop half of the whites into the large bowl and fold in, then scoop the rest of the whites and fold until there are no more streaks. Scrape the batter into the prepared pan and wiggle the pan to even it out.

**Make the topping:** In a small bowl, pinch together the garlic, rosemary, olive oil, and red pepper to coat. Sprinkle over the top of the batter.

Slide the pan into the oven and set a timer for 30 minutes. (If you're using a 9-inch cake pan, set the timer for 25 minutes.) Slide a toothpick into the center of the bread. If it comes out clean or with a few crumbs, you're good. If not, set a timer for 5 minutes and test again. Set aside to cool completely in the pan, about 1 hour. Use an offset spatula or butter knife to slide under and tilt the bread out of the pan, so you can get it onto a serving plate without ruining the topping.

## PARTY TRICKS

- Cover the top of the pan with aluminum foil if you're traveling with it. It can be served at room temperature or rewarmed in a 300°F oven for 10 minutes.

- Any leftover bread can be stored in a zip-top bag at room temperature for up to 2 days.

LIL
SWEETIES

**"JUST BRING DESSERT!"** can feel like one of the most horrifying sentences in the world. Like many of us, I spent years thinking I couldn't bake when, in reality, I just didn't know *how* to bake. Big difference! This chapter covers the MVP sweets—cookies, bars, pie, ice cream—in easy to nail recipes, so you can always feel like you have dessert covered.

# Mosaic Jell-O

ROLL UP YOUR SLEEVES | GF, NF

*Start this recipe 2 days ahead.*

What started as a Jell-O ad in the 1950s has evolved into the Mexican masterpiece gelatina de mosaico, a more gorgeous way of saying mosaic gelatin. It's an easy preparation of multicolored squares of cut-up Jell-O get mixed into a beautiful, milky-white cloak of gelatin, so they're suspended like a mosaic or stained glass. My friend Vivian Bond is a Jell-O fanatic, and I'll never forget her eyes popping out of her head when I brought over this dessert-as-sculpture showpiece. If Jell-O is a perfect summer dessert (and it is, please don't argue with me), then this is the perfect way to present it.

**Makes 1 Bundt, enough for 10 people**

3 (3-ounce) boxes Jell-O, in different flavors and colors
7 packets unflavored gelatin (see Party Tricks)
Nonstick cooking spray
½ cup cold water
1 (12-ounce) can evaporated milk
Whole milk
1 (14-ounce) can sweetened condensed milk
1 tablespoon pure vanilla extract

Arrange your Jell-O flavors from lightest to darkest color. (This way you can do one batch right after the other without having to stop and wash your bowl.) Starting with the lightest, pour the powder into a medium bowl. Add 1 packet of unflavored gelatin and whisk until they're combined. Boil water, then measure out 1 cup and pour it into the bowl. Whisk until the powder is completely dissolved, then whisk in 1 cup very cold water. Pour the mixture into a quart container, cover, and refrigerate overnight so the Jell-O is completely set. Repeat with the other two boxes of Jell-O along with two more packets of unflavored gelatin.

The next day, run a paring knife lengthwise and crosswise in each container to cut the Jell-O into squares, then around the perimeter for an easier release. Use the knife to coax the Jell-O out and into a large bowl. It's totally fine if there are a few small bits, it'll just add to the mosaic effect. Take a moment here to very thoroughly coat a 10-inch Bundt pan (see Party Tricks) with nonstick spray, then flip it upside down in the sink so the spray evenly spreads without pooling in the bottom.

Pour ½ cup cold water into a medium saucepan. Pour the remaining four packets unflavored gelatin into the saucepan and whisk a couple times to mix. Set a timer for 5 minutes, or until the gelatin has hydrated into a solid mass. Pour in the evaporated milk. Fill the empty can halfway with whole milk (that's ¾ cup, to be precise) and pour that in, too. Set the saucepan over low heat. At first nothing will happen, but after about 1 minute you should be able to start slowly whisking as the gelatin melts into the milk. Keep whisking for about 2 more minutes, until you have a completely smooth milk mixture. Remove from

*Recipe continues*

the stove and whisk in the condensed milk and vanilla. Let the mixture cool completely, about 15 minutes, then whisk again.

Flip the Bundt right-side up. Scatter a layer of Jell-O cubes along the bottom of the pan, mixing up the colors as you go, then ladle in the milk mixture until it's almost covered. Keep alternating Jell-O and milk, but take it slow because each layer of Jell-O is going to displace the milk and make it rise farther up the pan. Fill almost to the top, leaving about ½ inch of space. Cover the pan tightly with aluminum foil and carefully slide it into the refrigerator. Let it set overnight again.

To make sure the mold releases easily, fill a large bowl with warm water and slowly dip the Bundt in so the water comes about halfway up the sides. Hold it there for 2 or 3 seconds, then pat the outside of the Bundt dry, especially inside the center tube. Put the Bundt in one hand and set the serving plate on top, making sure it's centered. Put your other hand on top of the plate and quickly flip. If the mold doesn't drop onto the plate (It will! But just in case!), don't panic. Lightly tap the plate on the counter. If that fails (It won't! But just in case!), flip it back over, and take another dip in the water. Serve with a pie server or knife so everyone can cut their own slice.

## PARTY TRICKS

- Look for the 1-ounce box of Knox unflavored gelatin next to the Jell-O. Each one has four packets in it, so get two boxes.

- This recipe will work great with a small Bundt; just stop when it's full. It could also be done in a large bowl and presented as one big round.

- Cover any leftover Jell-O with plastic wrap and refrigerate for up to 1 week.

# Buttermilk Brownies

ROLL UP YOUR SLEEVES | VG, NF

These brownies not only have a splash of buttermilk inside to help make them extra soft and gooey, they also have a beautiful swirl of buttermilk, which makes them feel a hundred times more impressive than standard-issue brownies. All that buttermilk also gives a pleasant tartness to help balance all the chocolaty sweetness.

**Makes 9 brownies**

Nonstick cooking spray

BROWNIES
1 (4-ounce) sweet or
  bittersweet chocolate bar
½ cup (1 stick) unsalted butter
1 teaspoon instant espresso
  powder
1 cup (200 grams) sugar
½ cup (130 grams) buttermilk,
  very cold
2 large eggs
½ teaspoon kosher salt
1 cup (140 grams) all-purpose
  flour

TOPPING
2 tablespoons buttermilk
2 tablespoons milk powder or
  buttermilk powder

PARTY TRICK
• Leftover brownies can be
  stored in a zip-top bag at room
  temperature for up to 3 days.

Preheat the oven to 350°F and set a rack in the center. Coat an 8-inch (or 9-inch) square baking pan with nonstick spray. Measure two 10-inch pieces of parchment. Fold each in half lengthwise and press them into the baking pan in both directions so there's a little overhang on each side. (Metal binder clips are super helpful for keeping the parchment in place.) Coat the parchment with a little more spray, too.

**Make the brownies:** Set the chocolate bar on a large cutting board and use a serrated knife to cut diagonally across the bar. Rotate the cutting board a quarter turn and cut diagonally in the other direction to create small pieces. Cut the butter in half lengthwise, then cut across into 8 equal pieces. Scrape the butter and chocolate into a medium saucepan and add the espresso powder.

Set the saucepan over low heat. Use a whisk to stir occasionally as the butter and chocolate start melting. When they're about 75 percent melted, remove from the stove and let the residual heat finish the job. Whisk in the sugar and cold buttermilk until completely combined. Add the eggs and salt and quickly whisk it all together. Add the flour and switch to a rubber spatula to fold, really getting around the sides and bottom, until it's just combined but not overly mixed. Scrape the batter into the prepared baking pan.

**Make the topping:** Rinse off your whisk and spatula. In a small bowl, whisk the buttermilk and milk powder together to make a thick paste. Use the spatula to scrape into a small zip-top bag. Snip a tiny bit off the corner and slowly squeeze the paste across the brownie batter. Use a toothpick or cake tester to run swipes through the batter in the opposite direction, creating beautiful streaks. Rinse off that toothpick, we'll need it again!

Slide the pan into the oven and set a timer for 25 minutes. (If you're using a 9-inch cake pan, set the timer for 20 minutes.) When the timer goes off, insert the toothpick 1 inch from the edge. If it comes out clean or with a couple crumbs, you're good. If not, give it 5 more minutes, then check again. Cool in the pan for 30 minutes, then use the parchment slings to transfer to the cutting board. Slide the parchment out from underneath, then use the serrated knife to slice into 9 equal squares.

# Mango + Sticky Rice Pudding

IN YOUR SLEEP | V, GF, NF

**Growing up, I was obsessed with the Thai restaurant in my hometown, mostly because of the sole dessert option: mango and sticky rice. It's such a simple pairing that's somehow so perfect, and I could happily eat it every day. This rice pudding version is batched to a sharable quantity but keeps the spirit with bites of coconut-soaked rice and sweet, creamy, ripe mango.**

**Serves 8 people**

1 cup sticky rice (see Party Tricks)
3 (13.5-ounce) cans coconut milk (shake really well before opening!)
1 cup milk, unsweetened vegan or full-fat dairy
¾ cup sugar
1 teaspoon kosher salt
2 tablespoons unsalted butter, vegan or not
Chopped mango (see Party Tricks)
1 tablespoon toasted sesame seeds

In a heatproof medium bowl, use your hands to swish the rice in plenty of water to remove excess starch. Tilt the bowl to drain, pressing your hand against the rice to keep it in place. Do that two more times. Bring 3 cups water to a ripping boil, then pour it over the rice. Cover the bowl with a pot lid or large plate and set a timer for 30 minutes. Then run cold water into the bowl to cool and drain the rice one more time.

In a large saucepan, combine the rice, 2 cans of the coconut milk, the other milk, sugar, and salt. Bring to a boil over high heat, then reduce to medium-low and set a timer for 30 minutes. Stir consistently for the first 10 minutes; we don't want any rice getting stuck to the bottom and agitation will release the remaining starches and make the pudding creamy. After 10 minutes, you can move to an occasionally-to-often stir rhythm.

When the liquid has reduced and the rice is getting thick, around the 20-minute mark, add the remaining coconut milk. Simmer, stirring, until the timer goes off. Taste a few pieces of rice to make sure they're creamy and cooked through. If not, give it 5 more minutes. Stir in the butter until completely melted, then remove from the stove and cover. Set a timer for 10 minutes. When the timer goes off, fold in the mango.

Scrape the rice pudding into a large bowl or a 9 by 13-inch baking pan and smooth the top. Press plastic wrap directly on the surface and let cool for 1 hour, then refrigerate for at least 2 hours or up to 2 days. Just before serving, blanket the top with toasted sesame seeds.

## PARTY TRICKS

- Sticky rice is labeled as either sticky, sweet, or glutinous rice. If you can't find it, jasmine rice can step in for a floral experience.

- A 10-ounce bag of frozen mango chunks (no need to thaw), two 15-ounce cans of diced mango (drained and rinsed), or two fresh ripe mangoes work here.

- Any leftover rice pudding can be covered and refrigerated for up to 4 days.

*Apple + Chinese
Five-Spice Pie,
164*

# Blackberry + Basil Pie

IN YOUR SLEEP | VG, NF (V, GF)

For the story of this pie, flip to the Apple + Chinese Five-Spice Pie (page 164). Because the apple pie has a very traditional double crust, I wanted to offer a second, far-easier option. A press-in crust is exactly what it sounds like: a soft dough that you press directly into the pie plate, no rolling necessary, with an even easier crumb topping to blanket the fruit. Both crust options can be used interchangeably for both pies. But if you're new to baking, this crust is a perfect place to start.

**Makes one 9-inch pie**

PRESS-IN CRUST

4 tablespoons unsalted butter (see Party Tricks)
1½ cups (210 grams) all-purpose flour
¼ cup (50 grams) granulated sugar
1 teaspoon kosher salt
1 teaspoon baking powder

FILLING

12 ounces fresh blackberries
12 fresh basil leaves
¼ cup (50 grams) granulated sugar
2 tablespoons cornstarch
¼ teaspoon kosher salt

CRUMB TOPPING

1 cup (140 grams) all-purpose flour
¼ cup (55 grams) light brown sugar
¼ cup (50 grams) granulated sugar
¼ teaspoon kosher salt
4 tablespoons unsalted butter

Store-bought or homemade ice cream (page 179) or Maple Whipped Cream (page 207), for serving (both optional)

Melt the butter in a small bowl in the microwave, or in a small saucepan over low heat. Let it sit to cool to room temperature, about 10 minutes.

**Make the crust:** In a medium bowl, whisk the flour, sugar, salt, and baking powder until combined. Pour in the cooled butter plus ¼ cup very cold water. Use a rubber spatula to lightly mix until the dough starts to stick together and there are no dry crumbs. The dough should easily hold together without feeling sticky. If it still seems a little dry, mix in more cold water 1 teaspoon at a time. If it's way too sticky, mix in more flour 1 teaspoon at a time. When you get a cohesive dough, set a timer for 5 minutes and let the dough hydrate.

Use your hands to break the dough into 2 equal-ish pieces. Working with the first piece, crumble it into smaller pieces and scatter them around the bottom of a 9-inch pie plate. Press the pieces back together into an even crust across the bottom of the plate. Crumble the second piece evenly around the edge of the plate and press up the sides until it just peeks over the top by about ½ inch. (Keep that mixing bowl handy, we'll use it again.) Use a thumb and index finger on the outer perimeter and your other index finger on the inner perimeter. Rotate the pie plate as you work your way around, pressing the inner finger between the outer fingers to make a nice and even crimp. Loosely cover the dough with plastic wrap and place in the refrigerator. Set a timer for 30 minutes.

While the dough is chilling, preheat the oven to 425°F and set a rack in the lowest position.

**Next, make the filling:** I like to remove the paper liner from the blackberry containers (or any berry container), then keep the fruit in the container to rinse under cold water and drain. On a small cutting board, stack the basil leaves on top of one another, then roll the stack into a fat cigar. Slice across the tube to make long, thin basil ribbons.

*Recipe continues*

In that medium bowl you kept handy, whisk the sugar, cornstarch, and salt together. Add the berries and basil and use your hands to toss everything together. Let the fruit sit while the crust finishes chilling.

When the timer goes off, remove the plate from the fridge and discard the plastic. Use a rubber spatula to scrape the berry mixture into the crust and smooth into an even layer. The fruit might have just started releasing juices, so pour that in, too, if it's there. Wipe the bowl with a paper towel if there was any juice because we're about to use it again!

**Make the crumb topping:** In our heroic bowl, whisk the flour, brown sugar, granulated sugar, and salt together. Melt the butter, immediately pour it in, and use the rubber spatula to start mixing. Switch to your hands and pinch the mixture together into various-sized crumbs. If it's a little dry, add 1 tablespoon of warm water and keep pinching. Scatter the crumbs evenly over the top of the pie.

Place the pie plate on a rimmed baking sheet and slide onto the low rack. As soon as the pie is in, set a timer for 15 minutes. When the timer goes off, remove the pie from the oven and cover the entire top with aluminum foil. Reduce the oven temperature again to 375°F and put the pie back in. Set a timer for 50 minutes, but sneak a look at the pie periodically. When it's ready the filling will be bubbling away and slightly reduced, and the crust and crumb will be beautifully golden brown. Let the pie cool on a wire rack for at least 4 hours before serving with ice cream or maple whipped cream, if you want.

## PARTY TRICKS

- See Party Tricks on page 167 for adjustments to make a vegan and gluten-free pie dough. For the crumb topping in this recipe, King Arthur's Measure for Measure or Bob's Red Mill 1 to 1 can be used with any brand of vegan butter.

- Once the pie is cool, you can lightly wrap it in plastic and keep it at room temperature for up to 2 days. Leftovers can be wrapped and refrigerated for 2 more days.

# Milk + Cookies

IN YOUR SLEEP | VG, NF (GF)

A lot of digital and actual ink has been spilled on the ins and outs of chocolate chip cookies. But the thing no one talks about is the final touch, the Shaggy to the Scooby, the Thelma to the Louise. THE MILK! What I'm saying is *If You Give a Mouse a Cookie* was written about me, so don't even think about handing me a warm chocolate chip cookie if there's not a cold glass of milk to go with it. My friend Emily DePaula once showed up to a movie night with warm cookies and a gallon of milk and it was so effortlessly cool, I still haven't recovered. May we all bring that air to every party we grace with these cookies. (AND MILK!)

### Makes 14 cookies

½ cup (1 stick) unsalted butter
1 cup (200 grams) granulated sugar
1 cup packed (215 grams) dark brown sugar
1 teaspoon kosher salt
2 teaspoons milk powder
1 teaspoon baking powder
1 teaspoon baking soda
2 teaspoons pure vanilla extract
2 large eggs
2½ cups (350 grams) all-purpose flour (see Party Trick)
1 (12-ounce) bag semisweet chocolate chips
Half gallon milk, very cold (not optional)

### SPECIAL EQUIPMENT
2-ounce (¼-cup) cookie scoop (see Party Trick)

Preheat the oven to 350°F and set a rack in the center. Line two rimmed baking sheets with parchment paper.

In a large saucepan, set the butter over low heat to start melting. When it's about 50 percent melted, remove from the stove and let the residual heat finish the job. Add the granulated sugar, dark brown sugar, and salt; whisk into a thick, soft paste. Add the milk powder, baking powder, baking soda, vanilla, and eggs and immediately whisk. Keep whisking until it's nice and light.

Add the flour and chocolate chips. Switch to the rubber spatula and fold, really getting around the sides and bottom, until it's just combined but not overly mixed.

Use a cookie scoop to portion 6 generously rounded scoops of dough onto one of the prepared baking sheets, leaving 2 inches between each scoop. Slide it into the oven and set a timer for 16 minutes, turning the sheet around at 8 minutes, until the edges are brown but the centers are just barely set. While that first batch bakes, scoop the second batch on the other baking sheet and slide it in as soon as the first one comes out. (And remember to set your timer!)

Let the cookies cool completely on the sheet, about 1 hour. You can serve the cookies at room temp, but I really think they should be warmed up. Arrange half of the cookies on a parchment-lined baking sheet and slide into a 300°F oven for 5 minutes. (As always, ask your host if you can borrow a baking sheet, parchment, and oven space ahead of time!) Serve those cookies with tall glasses of cold milk for dunking, then warm up the second half.

### PARTY TRICK

- For a gluten-free version, an easy solution if you don't have a cookie scoop, and storage instructions, see Party Tricks on page 172.

# Apple + Chinese Five-Spice Pie

ROLL UP YOUR SLEEVES | VG, NF (V, GF)

*Optional: Start this recipe 1 day ahead.*

Years ago, my friend and the best host I've ever seen, Patrick Janelle, hosted a pie competition in his backyard. (Can you imagine a dreamier party?!) I entered this pie and the Blackberry + Basil Pie (page 159). The group of judges awarded the Blackberry + Basil second place (I lost to Alison Roman, lol) and this Apple + Chinese Five-Spice Pie won as the audience favorite. Ever since that day, I've been keeping these two pies very close to my chest, just on the off chance I ever wrote a cookbook. And lucky me, it's time to spill the pies! Chinese five-spice is a blend of anise, cinnamon, cloves, fennel, and either pepper or ginger, depending on the brand. I love how it provides a few of the spices you'd expect in an apple pie, while slipping in a couple exciting wildcards.

## Makes one 9-inch pie

### TRADITIONAL DOUBLE CRUST

2½ cups (350 grams) all-purpose flour (see Party Tricks), plus more for rolling

2 tablespoons sugar

1 teaspoon kosher salt

4 tablespoons cold Crisco (preferably from baking sticks)

1 cup (2 sticks) unsalted butter, cold (see Party Tricks)

### FILLING

6 large Honeycrisp, Gala, or Fuji apples (8 ounces each)

6 tablespoons apple cider vinegar

1 cup (200 grams) sugar

¼ cup (30 grams) cornstarch

1 teaspoon kosher salt

4 tablespoons unsalted butter

2 tablespoons Chinese five-spice (see Party Tricks)

1 large egg

Demerara or granulated sugar, for topping

Store-bought or homemade ice cream (page 179) or Maple Whipped Cream (page 207), for serving (both optional)

**Make the crust:** Pour ½ cup cold water into a small bowl and set in the freezer to chill.

In a food processor, pulse the flour, sugar, and salt a couple times to mix. Use a paring knife to cut the Crisco into tablespoon chunks and drop into the food processor. Process for about 15 seconds, until it's completely mixed in. Cut the butter into tablespoon chunks and drop them into the food processor. Pulse about 10 times, until the butter is broken down and the dough is in small to medium crumbles. (This can also be done by hand in a large bowl. Swirl the flour, sugar, and salt together, pinch in the Crisco until it's combined, pinch in the butter to make crumbles, then continue with the water.)

Tap the mixture into a large bowl. Spoon 6 tablespoons of the chilled water around the bowl, then use your hands to lightly mix until the dough starts to stick together and there are no dry crumbs. The dough should feel just on the edge of wet but not overly sticky. If it still seems a little dry, mix in more water 1 tablespoon at a time. If it's way too sticky, mix in more flour 1 tablespoon at a time. When you have a cohesive, hydrated ball of dough, turn out onto the counter. Divide into two equal portions, pat into fat discs, wrap tightly in plastic wrap, and refrigerate (see Party Tricks).

When it's pie time, remove the discs from the fridge and set a timer for 10 minutes to let them warm up. Lightly flour your counter. Unwrap one of the discs, but keep the plastic nearby. Place the dough on the counter, sprinkle a little flour on top, and set your rolling pin in the center of the dough with your hands at three o'clock and nine o'clock. Gently roll up to the edge of the dough, then slide a hand under the dough and rotate it a quarter turn. Back to three

*Recipe continues*

and nine, roll up, rotate. Repeat this process, stopping to add more flour under or over the dough if it's sticky, or pinch together any cracks, until you have a 12-inch round.

Add a tiny bit of flour to the top of the dough and slide your pie plate nearby. Fold the dough in half, then in half again to make a triangle. Lift it and set the tip of the triangle in the center of the pie plate, then unfold your dough. Work your way around the plate, lifting the edge of the dough with one hand and easing it into the plate with the other, until it's fully touching the pie plate with some still hanging over. Lay the reserved plastic over the dough, including the overhang and pop the plate into the fridge to chill. Wipe the counter clean and lay out a 12-inch-long piece of parchment. Lightly dust the parchment with flour, unwrap the other disc of dough, and use the same process, except rotate the parchment instead of lifting the dough. Roll into a 12-inch circle again, then slide the parchment onto a rimmed baking sheet. Lay the plastic over the dough and slide into the refrigerator. Set a timer for 30 minutes.

**Now is a great time to make the filling:** Keep a large bowl nearby. Peel and cut the apples into ½-inch-thick slices. Scoop them into the bowl and toss with the apple cider vinegar.

Add the sugar, cornstarch, and salt to the bowl. In a small skillet, melt the butter over low heat. As soon as the butter is melted, pull it off the stove and sprinkle the five-spice over top. Whisk for 20 to 30 seconds, until the spices are super fragrant, then use a rubber spatula to scrape into the bowl and toss everything together.

When the timer goes off, pull the pie plate out of the fridge and discard the plastic. Use your hands to scoop and spread the apples into the pie plate, making a gorgeous rolling hill in the center. Pour any juices over top. Pull the baking sheet out of the fridge and discard the plastic. Fold the dough in fourths like we did for the pie plate, setting the tip in the center and unfolding.

We want a little overhang, about ½ inch, so use kitchen scissors to trim around if there's any egregious amounts. (But keep those scraps in case you need to patch up any areas!) Pinch the top and bottom crust to seal together, then roll the bottom crust up and over the top so the edge of the crust lies perfectly on the edge of the plate. Use a thumb and index finger on the outer perimeter and your other index finger on the inner perimeter. Rotate the pie plate as you work your way around, pressing the inner finger between the outer fingers to make a pretty little crimp. Return the pie to the refrigerator and set a timer for 45 minutes.

While the pie is chilling, preheat the oven. If your pie plate is metal, preheat to 425°F and set a rack in the lowest position. Line a rimmed baking sheet with aluminum foil and put it on the low rack to preheat. If your pie plate is glass, do the same thing but do not put your foil-lined baking sheet in the oven.

In a small bowl, whisk the egg with 1 tablespoon water and keep it nearby. Brush the top and edges of the crust with the egg wash, then generously sprinkle sugar over top. Use the paring knife to cut four 1-inch vents in the center of the crust. Place a metal pie plate on the preheated baking sheet, or a glass pie plate on the not preheated baking sheet, and slide onto the low rack. As soon as the pie is in, set a timer for 25 minutes. When the timer goes off, reduce the oven temperature again to 375°F. It'll be another 30 to 40 minutes, so set a timer for 30 minutes to start, but sneak a look at the pie periodically. If the edges are browning too fast, remove the pie and gently pinch thin strips of tin foil around the crust, then slide it back in to keep baking. In the end you might be right on target, or you might need the extra time; the pie will be a deep golden brown all over and the filling will be bubbling away. Let the pie cool on a wire rack for at least 4 hours before serving with ice cream or maple whipped cream, if you want.

## PARTY TRICKS

- Gluten-free flour behaves a little differently in the context of pie dough, so, unfortunately, you won't be able to make a direct swap here. King Athur and Bob's Red Mill both make gluten-free pie dough mixes that produce two crusts, so those would be your best bet. Follow their package directions, not my recipe. This pie filling is already gluten-free.

- To make this vegan, swap the butter in the dough and filling for all Crisco. Baking sticks are really the way to go for the closest texture, and other vegan butters don't work as well. When it's time for the egg wash, whisk 2 tablespoons of vegan milk with 1 tablespoon of agave.

- Chinese five-spice is a spice blend that hits five key flavors: sweet, bitter, tart, salty, and savory. It's pretty common in grocery stores but would also be easy to find in an Asian market or online spice store.

- I'd love it if you did this the day before so the dough has plenty of time to chill, but 2 hours is fine if you're cramming. If you're really getting ahead of yourself, wrap the discs in plastic and then aluminum foil, label with a date, and freeze for up to 1 month. Thaw in the fridge overnight before using.

- Once the pie is cool, you can lightly wrap it in plastic and keep it at room temperature for up to 2 days. Leftovers can be wrapped and refrigerated for 2 more days.

# Party Krispies

A quick toss with some lightly browned butter and toasted coconut shreds gives these krispies an unusually great depth of flavor. We could stop right there, but where's the fun in that? What makes these party krispies is the no rules, no limits toppings as you pile on everything sweet and gorgeous and fun. There's a long list of my favorites in the ingredient list, and the only advice I have for you is to think strategically when you're planning out what to buy, keeping in mind that you ideally want a mix of colors, sizes, textures, flavors, and shapes for maximum impact.

## Makes 12 squares

Nonstick cooking spray
½ cup (1 stick) unsalted butter
1 cup unsweetened shredded coconut
1 (10-ounce) bag mini marshmallows
¼ teaspoon kosher salt
6 cups Rice Krispies (from a 12-ounce box; see Party Tricks)
Any combination of crushed mini pretzels, crushed potato chips, crushed Oreos, crushed frosted animal crackers, white chocolate chips, peanut butter chips, butterscotch chips, rainbow sprinkles, confetti sprinkles, decorative sprinkles, sparkling sugar, sanding sugar, edible glitter, Fruity Pebbles, Lucky Charms marshmallows, or flaky sea salt, for garnish

Coat a 9 by 13-inch baking pan with nonstick spray. Measure a 16-inch piece of parchment. Fold it in half lengthwise and press it lengthwise into the baking pan so there's a little overhang on each side. (Metal binder clips are super helpful for keeping the parchment in place.) Coat the parchment with a little more spray, too.

In a large Dutch oven (see Party Tricks), melt the butter over medium heat. Once the butter is melted, add the coconut and use a rubber spatula to coat in the butter. We're going to lightly toast the coconut and lightly brown the butter at the same time, so stay sharp. Let the mixture simmer and bubble, stirring occasionally. At about 4 minutes, it'll be pretty foamy. Start stirring continuously so you can see what's going on in there. Around 5 or 6 minutes in, the coconut will have a light golden toast and the butter will be tan.

Remove from the stove and immediately stir in the marshmallows and salt. Keep stirring until they're about 75 percent melted, then add the Rice Krispies. Very slowly and gently fold in the cereal as the marshmallows finish melting. (You'll hear some snap, crackle, and popping—totally normal.) Scrape into the prepared baking pan. Lightly coat a smaller piece of parchment with nonstick spray and use it to press the mixture into an evenly distributed rectangle (see Party Tricks). While it's still sticky, blanket the top with a mix of treats.

Slide the pan into the refrigerator for about 30 minutes to set. When the krispies feel firm, use the sling to lift them out of the pan and onto a large cutting board. Slide the parchment out from underneath, then slice into 12 equal squares. Arrange them on a serving platter or store somewhere cool until it's go time.

## PARTY TRICKS

- Rice Krispies are not gluten-free! A few brands are, like Nature's Path and One Degree Organic Foods. Just pay attention to your toppings if you're going GF.

- A light-colored enamel or stainless-steel pot will help you monitor the butter browning. Anything with a black surface will literally leave you in the dark.

- Leftover treats can be stored in a zip-top bag at room temperature for up to 3 days.

# Subway Cookies

If you're expecting a dupe of cookies from the sandwich place Subway, then I'm truly sorry I misled you. But the great news is these are even better. I call them Subway Cookies because years ago when I was first developing this recipe, I packed a batch up and took them on the New York City subway with me. The deep black cocoa against the brown chocolate chips makes these oddly striking in person—really, you'll be surprised—and the woman next to me was asking about them. After chatting for a minute, I asked, ". . . is this weird? Do you want one?" She quickly whipped out her empty meal prep container, and I gave her one. But when I cracked the lid open, the woman on my other side said, "Oh my god, those smell incredible. Can I buy one off you?" So I gave her one for free, and for a moment three jaded New Yorkers were giggling over cookies on the subway.

## Makes 12 cookies

½ cup (1 stick) unsalted butter

¼ cup (65 grams) creamy peanut butter (see Party Tricks)

½ cup (100 grams) granulated sugar

½ cup packed (110 grams) light brown sugar

1 teaspoon kosher salt

1 teaspoon pure vanilla extract

1 large egg

¼ cup (30 grams) black cocoa powder (see Party Tricks)

½ teaspoon baking soda

½ teaspoon baking powder

1 cup (140 grams) all-purpose flour

1 (12-ounce) bag semisweet chocolate chips

### SPECIAL EQUIPMENT

2-ounce (¼-cup) cookie scoop (see Party Tricks)

Preheat the oven to 350°F and set a rack in the center. Line two rimmed baking sheets with parchment paper.

In a large saucepan, combine the butter and peanut butter. Set over low heat and whisk occasionally as the butter and peanut butter melt together. When they're about 50 percent melted, remove from the stove and let the residual heat finish the job. Add the granulated sugar, brown sugar, and salt; whisk into a thick, soft paste. Add the vanilla and egg and immediately whisk. The mixture will seize up, but keep whisking until it's nice and light.

Add the black cocoa, baking soda, and baking powder. Switch to a rubber spatula and fold until completely combined into a glossy mixture. Add the flour and chocolate chips and fold, really getting around the sides and bottom, until it's just combined but not overly mixed.

Use a cookie scoop to portion five scoops of dough—scraping on the side of the bowl so it's a packed scoop—onto one of the prepared baking sheets, leaving 2 inches between each scoop. Slide the baking sheet into the oven and set a timer for 12 minutes, turning the sheet around at 6 minutes, until the cookies are puffy and slightly spread. While that first batch bakes, scoop the second batch on the other baking sheet and slide it in as soon as the first one comes out. (And remember to set your timer!)

*Recipe continues*

As soon as a sheet comes out of the oven, lift it a few inches above the counter and let it drop. Repeat two more times to flatten and spread the cookies, then let them cool completely on the sheet, about 1 hour. Repeat this process when the second sheet is done.

## PARTY TRICKS

- I've tried a lot of peanut butter brands in these cookies, and my favorite by far is the original Jif. (Skippy is a very close second!) You might be tempted to reach for natural peanut butter instead, but when it comes to baking, the oil in natural peanut butter is going to cause more spread, less lift, and an unreliable texture.

- Black cocoa powder is different from regular and even Dutch-processed cocoa powder. It has a deep black color (Oreos use it!) and a complex dark chocolate punch. It's what really sets these cookies apart and can be easily purchased online. If it's just not in the cards, Hershey's Special Dark 100% cacao is a good substitute.

- King Arthur's Measure for Measure or Bob's Red Mill 1 to 1 work great here for a gluten-free version.

- If you don't have a cookie scoop, just measure ¼ cup into your palm and roll into a rough, imperfect ball.

- The cooled cookies can be stacked in large airtight containers or zip-top bags and stored at room temperature for up to 3 days.

# Raspberry Meringue Tart

BRAGGING RIGHTS | NF (GF)

*Optional: Start this recipe 1 day ahead.*

Somehow anything pressed into a tart pan comes out looking so professional when you slide the sides off. This easy cookie crust is no exception. Filled with a sweet-tart raspberry curd and finished with huge clouds of peaky Italian meringue, well, I'm not sure if I could ever go back to lemon. It's worth the small investment in a kitchen torch to get those dreamy browned edges that make a meringue pie so picture-perfect.

**Makes one 9-inch tart**

### CRUST
32 Biscoff cookies (250 grams) or other cookies (see Party Tricks)
¼ cup (30 grams) powdered sugar
6 tablespoons unsalted butter

### FILLING
16 ounces frozen raspberries
1 cup (200 grams) granulated sugar
¼ teaspoon kosher salt
3 large egg yolks (save those whites for the meringue!)
2 teaspoons cornstarch
1 (0.25-ounce) packet unflavored gelatin (from a 1-ounce box)
4 tablespoons unsalted butter, cut into 1-tablespoon pieces

### MERINGUE
1¼ cups (250 grams) granulated sugar
3 large egg whites
¼ teaspoon cream of tartar

### SPECIAL EQUIPMENT
9-inch tart pan
Stand mixer

Preheat the oven to 350°F and set a rack in the center.

**Start the crust:** Before it's out of commission, whirl your cookies in the food processor. Make sure you end up with 2 cups of fine crumbs—process more cookies if you need to. Cookies go in a large bowl, the food processor gets a quick rinse and snapped back into place.

**Make the filling:** In a medium saucepan, combine the raspberries, granulated sugar, salt, and ½ cup cold water. Set over medium heat, cover, and set a timer for 10 minutes. While that's simmering, whisk the egg yolks and cornstarch in a small bowl, then sprinkle the gelatin over top. When the timer goes off, ladle a little of the raspberry mixture into the egg mixture and whisk to combine, then pour it all back into the saucepan. Stir until the mixture starts to thicken, about 2 minutes, then scrape into the food processor. With the processor running, add the butter one piece at a time. Scrape down the sides and process for 30 more seconds to make sure everything is combined. Keep the lid on the processor and set a timer for 1 hour to let it cool.

While the filling is cooling, let's come back to the crust: Whisk the powdered sugar into the cookie crumbs. Melt the butter and drizzle it into the cookie bowl. Mix until the crumbs are hydrated. Eyeball about two-thirds of the mixture and sprinkle that over the bottom of a 9-inch tart pan. Press into an even layer. Sprinkle the rest of the mixture around the edges of the pan and press to make the sides. Do another press around to make sure there are no cracks or uneven patches. Slide the crust in the oven and set a timer for 10 minutes. Remove and very gently press a measuring cup around the edges to make sure the crust perfectly cools in all the nooks and crannies. Cool completely while the filling finishes setting up. (We're done with the oven, you can turn it off.)

*Recipe continues*

When the hour is up, the filling should have a skin on top and still be very warm. Process again, just for 30 seconds. Hold a medium mesh strainer over the crust and pour the filling in. Give the pan just the tiniest littlest wiggle to help the filling settle in an even layer, then press plastic wrap directly on the surface. Set a timer for 2 hours and let the filling set at room temperature, then transfer to the refrigerator for another 2 hours or up to 24 hours.

**When it's getting close to go time, make the meringue:** Set a small saucepan on the stove and attach a thermometer. Pour in the granulated sugar, then slowly pour in ½ cup cold water. Don't stir or move the saucepan. Set over high heat and let the sugar melt on its own and boil. It's ready when the thermometer hits 240°F.

Before that happens, put the egg whites in the bowl of a stand mixer fitted with the whisk attachment. Beat on low for about 1 minute, until they're foamy. Add the cream of tartar, then increase the speed to medium and whip until the whites are fluffy and soft peaks form, about 2 minutes.

As soon as the sugar syrup hits 240°F, remove it from the stove. I like to pour mine into a liquid measuring cup because a pour spout makes all the difference for this next part. With the mixer running on low, very slowly pour the syrup down the side of the bowl until it's all mixed in. (You want to stream it down the side so it mixes with the egg whites instead of tussling with the whisk.) Increase the speed to high and whip until the sides of the bowl are back to room temperature and the meringue is at stiff peaks, around 8 minutes.

Scoop and swirl the meringue into a big pile over the top of the tart. It's beautiful in its glossy, snowy whiteness, but if you have a kitchen torch, singe the meringue for a perfectly toasted finish. If you're not serving it within the next hour, store it in the refrigerator for up to 4 hours. To serve, center the base of the tart pan on a can of beans or something small with some height and slide the side down to remove. You can serve straight from the base of the pan or carefully slide the tart onto a serving plate.

## PARTY TRICKS

- See Party Tricks on page 100 for a list of my favorite cookie options.
- Any leftovers can be wrapped and refrigerated for 2 more days.

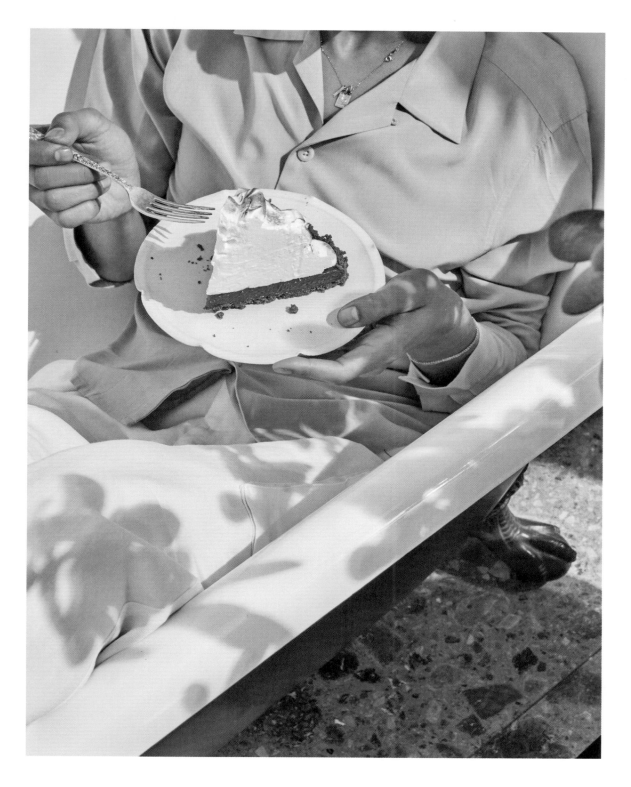

# Very Creamy Ice Cream

ROLL UP YOUR SLEEVES | VG, GF, NF

*Start this recipe at least 1 day ahead.*

As soon as the weather was even a little humid, my family would drag a tub-size ice cream maker out onto the back deck, fill it with ice and rock salt, let it churn away, rinse, and repeat all summer. So you'll understand why it's very hard for me to not have just a little bite of ice cream at the end of a hot night. The common pitfall of homemade ice cream is it can become a little too icy and not creamy enough, but this recipe makes a foolproof base that stays *so* velvety even after weeks in the freezer. And because we're already working with a sweet cream base, I riffed on three classic drinks—Orange Julius, Iced Coffee, Taro Milk Tea—plus bonus tips to guide you toward the more classic flavors.

## Makes 2 pints, plus a little extra treat for you

5 large egg yolks (save the whites for Brown Sugar Angel, page 205)
¾ cup (150 grams) sugar
1 tablespoon light corn syrup (see Party Tricks)
½ teaspoon kosher salt
1½ cups (345 grams) whole milk
1½ cups (350 grams) heavy cream
Ice
Flavors (see chart, page 180)

### SPECIAL EQUIPMENT

Candy or deep-fry thermometer (see Party Tricks)
Ice cream maker

Set your ice cream maker parts in the freezer to start chilling.

In a medium saucepan, whisk the yolks to break them up. Sprinkle the sugar over the yolks, add the corn syrup and salt, and whisk to incorporate. Whisk in the milk about a ½ cup at a time so the eggs get fully incorporated. Pour in the cream and switch to a rubber spatula. Give the sides and bottom a good scrape to mix in any stray egg or sugar. Attach the thermometer to the side of the saucepan.

Set a medium mesh strainer over a medium bowl and keep those close by. In the sink, fill a large bowl halfway with ice and cold water. Set the saucepan over low heat. Use the spatula to constantly stir and scrape along the bottom and sides to prevent scorching. Keep an eye on the thermometer—after 10 to 15 minutes it'll hit 170°F and the custard should be just slightly thickened. Pull it off the stove and pour through the strainer into the bowl. Even with the most careful mixing, you're going to catch a few egg curds; don't panic.

Remove the strainer and nestle the bowl into the ice water. Wash and dry your spatula, then set a timer for 10 minutes and occasionally stir the custard as it cools. Remove from the ice bath and press plastic wrap directly onto the surface of the custard and up the sides of the bowl. I like to tightly wrap the top of the bowl too, just to be safe. Transfer to the fridge for at least 8 hours, but preferably 24 hours.

Whisk the flavoring of your choice into the chilled custard, then pour it into the chilled ice cream maker. Churn until the ice cream is the texture of a thick soft serve—the timing of this will depend on your model, so trust your eyes.

*Recipe continues*

Remove the ice cream paddle, use a spatula to scrape it clean, then start scooping the ice cream into the pint containers, leaving about ½ inch of space at the top. (Any of the leftover soft serve is all yours!)

Press the lids on the pints. Use a Sharpie to write the flavor and a date 2 weeks from now on the top. Freeze the pints for at least 4 hours or overnight before serving. Let sit at room temp for 5 to 10 minutes before scooping.

| FLAVORS | |
| --- | --- |
| **ORANGE JULIUS** | ½ cup (120 grams) Tang drink mix |
| **ICED COFFEE** | 1 tablespoon instant coffee granules |
| **TARO MILK TEA** | 1 cup (170 g) taro powder mix |

### PARTY TRICKS

- It's okay, this is not *high-fructose* corn syrup. A little bit of light corn syrup is totally harmless and will make the finished ice cream unbelievably creamy. It also makes frosting dreamy and sauces glossy. Trust me, it's worth it.

- If you own an ice cream maker, I think you probably also own a thermometer. Unfortunately, there's not really a plan B here, so definitely get your hands on one before you start.

- The chart above has some flavors that have become my staples. If you're feeling less adventurous, churn as is for a great fior di latte. For classic vanilla, add 1 tablespoon pure vanilla extract, or vanilla bean paste for little flecks of seeds. For classic chocolate, chop and melt 8 ounces semisweet or bittersweet chocolate (see Party Tricks on page 199), then cool for 15 minutes before mixing into the base.

Orange
Julius

Iced
Coffee

Taro Milk
Tea

CAKED UP

BECAUSE DESSERT IS SO often requested, I'm devoting TWO WHOLE CHAPTERS to the topic! Coming over with a freshly baked cake is a dying artform and I for one will not go gentle into that good night. With a mix of styles, layers, and skill levels, there's something here for everyone. And unlike desserts (page 150)—which are for, well, dessert—cakes can be served as breakfast, afternoon snacks, or the perfect finale to a meal.

# Lemon Bar Cake

ROLL UP YOUR SLEEVES | VG, NF

My boyfriend, Pacifico, is obsessed with all things lemon, whether sweet, savory, or in between. So this cake, which is the baby of a classic gooey butter cake and a tart lemon bar, really makes him feral. I can't disagree. The base is a soft, almost shortbread texture just barely cradling a gooey filling that goes full tilt on sweet-sour lemon flavor. The major advantage to this being a cake instead of a bar is that a large piece is exactly the correct serving size.

**Makes a 9-inch cake**

Nonstick cooking spray

### CAKE
½ cup (1 stick) unsalted butter, melted
1 cup (200 grams) sugar
1 large lemon
1 large egg
2 teaspoons cream of tartar
1 teaspoon baking powder
½ teaspoon kosher salt
1¼ cups (175 grams) all-purpose flour

### FILLING
1 large lemon
1 teaspoon kosher salt
1 large egg
2 teaspoons cream of tartar
1 (8-ounce) block cream cheese, at room temperature
1 (16-ounce) box powdered sugar

### SPECIAL EQUIPMENT
9-inch (or 8-inch) springform pan

**Two hours before you start, pull the cream cheese out of the fridge to soften.**

**Make the cake:** Preheat the oven to 350°F and set a rack in the center. Lay a large piece of parchment over the base of a 9-inch (or 8-inch) springform pan, then set the springform ring on the base and snap it into place. I like the rustic look of the flowing parchment in the final presentation, but you can trim it to the edge of the pan if you want. Coat the pan and parchment with nonstick spray.

In a large bowl, whisk the butter and sugar until it pulls together. Zest the lemon directly into the bowl, add the egg, and whisk again. One more whisk for the cream of tartar, baking powder, and salt, then switch to a rubber spatula and fold in the flour. Scrape the dough into the prepared cake pan and press into an even layer.

**Make the filling:** In the same bowl, zest the lemon. Add the salt and use your fingers to pinch and rub until the mixture is super fragrant. Cut the lemon in half and squeeze the juice right in. Whisk in the egg, cream of tartar, and cream cheese until completely smooth. Scoop out 3 tablespoons of the powdered sugar into a small bowl and set it aside for dusting the cake. Pour the rest of the powdered sugar into the filling bowl and whisk to combine.

Scrape the filling into the center of the cake pan. Wiggle the pan once or twice to help it spread toward the edges. Slide the cake into the oven and set a timer for 40 minutes. (If you're using an 8-inch pan, set the timer for 45 minutes.) The edge of the cake will be nicely golden brown and the center will be bubbly and lightly browned all over. Add 5 more minutes to the timer if it needs it. Cool for 15 minutes, then run a butter knife around the perimeter of the pan to make sure the edges don't stick. Keep cooling the cake in the pan for another 45 minutes, then cover the top of the pan with plastic wrap and refrigerate for at

*Recipe continues*

least 2 hours or overnight. Let the cake sit at room temperature for at least 1 hour before serving.

To serve, unlatch and remove the spring from. I like to serve the cake right on the base with a skirt of parchment, but you can run an offset spatula under the cake to release and transfer to a platter. Either way, dust the cake with the reserved powdered sugar before serving.

## PARTY TRICKS

- For a super clean slice, run a knife under hot water for a few seconds, then wipe dry with a kitchen towel. It'll slide right through the cake.

- Leftover cake can be covered and refrigerated for up to 3 days.

# Pumpkin Carrot Cake

ROLL UP YOUR SLEEVES | VG (NF)

*Optional: Start this recipe 1 day ahead.*

I don't know why, but everyone has *strong* opinions about what goes in a carrot cake, and do you know what I'd love more than anything else? If you kept that info to yourself! This recipe has walnuts. If that stirs up something in you, leave them out. Are you team raisins or pro-coconut? Bring them in. This is your varsity squad, and you can make the cuts. The one addition no one saw coming (even me, until I was one recipe over in my manuscript and mashed two together, lol) is pumpkin puree. But the exciting news is a can of pumpkin mixed in adds excellent flavor, great color, and so much moisture, and it can exist with all the same flavors that would already be in a carrot cake. Now that I've tried it, I will never turn back!

## Makes a 9-inch cake

Nonstick cooking spray

### CAKE
3 or 4 large carrots (8 ounces total)
1½ cups packed (320 grams) dark brown sugar
¼ cup (60 grams) vegetable oil
2 large eggs
1 cup packed (240 grams) pumpkin puree (see Party Tricks)
1 tablespoon pumpkin pie spice (see Party Tricks)
½ teaspoon baking powder
½ teaspoon baking soda
1 teaspoon kosher salt
1½ cups (210 grams) all-purpose flour
1 cup (110 grams) roughly chopped walnuts (optional)

### SPECIAL EQUIPMENT
9-inch (or 8-inch) springform pan

**Make the cake:** Preheat the oven to 350°F and set a rack in the center. Coat a 9-inch (or 8-inch) springform pan with nonstick spray.

Peel the carrots and run them over the large holes of a box grater. Stop when you need to, the safety of your fingers is very important to me.

In a large bowl, whisk the sugar and vegetable oil until combined. Add the eggs one at a time and whisk hard to add a lot of air to the mixture until it's light and fluffy, about 3 minutes. Whisk in the pumpkin puree until it's combined, then the pumpkin spice, baking powder, baking soda, and salt. Switch to a rubber spatula to fold in the flour, grated carrots, and walnuts, if you want to use them.

Scrape the batter into the prepared pan and smooth the top. Slide it into the oven and set a timer for 50 minutes. (If you're using an 8-inch pan, set the timer for 55 minutes.) Slide a toothpick into the center of the cake. If it comes out clean or with a few crumbs, you're good. If not, set a timer for 5 minutes and test again. Let the finished cake cool for 15 minutes, then run a butter knife around the perimeter of the pan to make sure the edges don't stick. Finish cooling completely in the pan, about 2 hours. (And before you step away, set out the butter and cream cheese to soften for the frosting!)

**When the cake is cool, make the frosting:** In a medium bowl, use a handheld mixer (or stand mixer with the whisk) to beat the powdered sugar and softened butter on low to combine. Stop and use a rubber spatula to scrape the sides and bottom of the bowl. Add the cream cheese, vanilla, and salt, then mix on low until combined. Increase the speed to medium-high and whip for a

*Ingredients and recipe continue*

## FROSTING

1½ cups (180 grams) powdered sugar

½ cup (1 stick) unsalted butter, at room temperature

4 ounces cream cheese, cut into cubes and chilled

1 teaspoon pure vanilla extract

¼ teaspoon kosher salt

½ cup pepitas

minute or two, until the frosting is fluffy and thick. Refrigerate the frosting for 15 minutes before spreading.

Spread the pepitas in a small skillet and set over low heat. Toss or stir occasionally as they warm up, until they're fragrant but not browned, about 3 minutes. Pour them into a small bowl to cool.

At this point you can unlatch and remove the springform. Slide an offset spatula or butter knife under the cake and rotate the base to release the cake. Slide the cake onto a serving plate. Use the offset or a regular spatula to scoop and smooth the frosting over the top of the cake, leaving a ½-inch border around the perimeter and flicking some waves over the surface. Sprinkle the pepitas evenly around the edge of the frosting before serving.

### PARTY TRICKS

- I've tried a lot of brands of pumpkin puree and Libby's is the best, no competition!

- If you don't have pumpkin spice, mix 1 teaspoon ground cinnamon, 1 teaspoon ground ginger, and ½ teaspoon each ground nutmeg and ground cloves. Or 2½ teaspoons Chinese five-spice would also be a killer substitute.

- If you want to start this recipe a day early, transfer the frosting to an airtight container and refrigerate overnight, then let it sit at room temperature for 30 minutes before spreading. Cover the cake pan with plastic and let sit overnight. If you're traveling with this cake, you can either assemble and frost at home or stack your serving plate on top of the springform and bring all the pieces with you to assemble there.

- Leftover cake can be covered and refrigerated for up to 3 days.

Easy Apple
Cake, 193

# Easy Apple Cake

IN YOUR SLEEP | VG, NF

I grew up in New England, where fall is a personality trait. When I was little, we would go to a farm in rural New Hampshire that offered hayrides and the best apple cake I've ever had in my life. When the air gets chilly and the apples are ripe for the picking, this is all I want to eat. The batter is what you'd expect, with diced apples, sour cream, and cinnamon, plus a crunchy topping of chopped walnuts and brown sugar. But the curveball here is apple cider vinegar, which not only adds a ton of great apple flavor, but also gives the cake a lofty, fluffy lift.

**Makes a 9-inch cake**

Nonstick cooking spray

### CAKE
½ cup (1 stick) unsalted butter, at room temperature (to soften quickly, see Party Tricks on page 202)
1 cup (200 grams) granulated sugar
2 large eggs
½ cup (120 grams) sour cream
2 tablespoons (30 grams) apple cider vinegar
1 teaspoon baking powder
1 teaspoon kosher salt
1 teaspoon ground cinnamon
1 teaspoon pure vanilla extract
2 cups (280 grams) all-purpose flour
3 large Honeycrisp, Gala, or Fuji apples, peeled and diced into ½-inch cubes

### TOPPING
½ cups (110 grams) dark brown sugar
½ cup (55 grams) roughly chopped walnuts
1 teaspoon ground cinnamon
Powdered sugar or Maple Whipped Cream (page 207), for serving (optional)

### SPECIAL EQUIPMENT
9-inch (or 8-inch) springform pan

Preheat the oven to 350°F and set a rack in the center. Coat a 9-inch (or 8-inch) springform pan with nonstick spray. Set the pan on a rimmed baking sheet to be safe.

In a large bowl, whisk the butter and granulated sugar until combined. Add the eggs one at a time and whisk hard to add a lot of air to the mixture until it's light and fluffy, about 2 minutes. Whisk in the sour cream and vinegar, and then the baking powder, salt, cinnamon, and vanilla. Switch to a rubber spatula to fold in the flour and apple pieces until just combined.

Scrape the batter into the prepared pan and smooth the top. In a small bowl, pinch the brown sugar, walnuts, and cinnamon together to combine, then sprinkle evenly over the batter. Slide the cake into the oven and set a timer for 50 minutes. (If you're using an 8-inch pan, set the timer for 55 minutes.) The cake should be golden brown and a toothpick inserted in the center should come out clean or with a few crumbs. If not, set a timer for 5 more minutes and check again.

Cool the cake in the pan, about 1 hour, then run an offset spatula (or butter knife) or around the rim before releasing. Slide the offset spatula under the bottom of the cake, too, then use it plus another wider spatula to slide the cake onto a serving plate. Maybe dust the top with powdered sugar before slicing and serving, maybe top with whipped cream, maybe enjoy on its own.

## PARTY TRICKS

- If you're traveling with this cake, you can cool completely or head out while it's still cooling. Either way, keep it in the pan and cover it with a kitchen towel. Bring a serving plate with you.

- Leftover cake can be covered and left at room temperature for up to 3 days or refrigerated for up to 5 days.

# Peach + Ginger Upside-Down Cake

ROLL UP YOUR SLEEVES | VG, NF (GF)

This lightly ginger-spiced cake is the perfect base (well, topping that later becomes a base) for juicy, ripe peaches. Of course, I've made the cake with frozen peaches, but it really is next level if you can wait for summer when they're plump and perfect. Ground ginger is not only a lot easier than grating fresh or chopping candied, it also packs a big ginger punch, which is my partner of choice all the time for peaches. It's one of those back-pocket, seemingly effortless cakes that our grandmothers all somehow had, and it's especially perfect outside on a humid night.

**Makes an 8-inch cake**

Nonstick cooking spray

PEACHES

2 tablespoons unsalted butter, melted
½ cup (100 grams) sugar
2 teaspoons cornstarch
2 teaspoons ground ginger powder
¼ teaspoon kosher salt
1 pound ripe peaches (see Party Tricks)

CAKE

¾ cup (150 grams) sugar
½ cup (1 stick) unsalted butter, at room temperature (see Party Trick on page 202)
2 large eggs
½ cup (120 grams) sour cream
2 teaspoons ground ginger
2 teaspoons ground cinnamon
½ teaspoon kosher salt
1 teaspoon almond extract (optional)
½ teaspoon baking powder
¼ teaspoon baking soda
1½ cups (210 grams) all-purpose flour (see Party Tricks)
Maple Whipped Cream (page 207), for serving (optional)

Preheat the oven to 350°F and set a rack in the lower third. Set an 8-inch (or 9-inch) cake pan right-side up on a piece of parchment. Trace around the bottom of the pan, then cut around the inside of the circle to avoid the ink. Coat the bottom and sides of the pan with nonstick spray, then press the parchment round to the bottom.

**Make the peaches:** Pour the melted butter into the bottom of the prepared pan and swirl to coat the parchment. In a small bowl, pinch the sugar, cornstarch, ginger, and salt together, then sprinkle evenly over the butter. Cut the peaches into ½-inch-thick slices. Lay the peach slices, slightly overlapping, in a circle around the rim of the pan, then another overlapping circle inside, then a few more pieces to cover the center. You'll probably have extra slices, so A) pick only the best ones for the pan and B) enjoy your snack.

**Make the cake:** In the bowl of a stand mixer fitted with the paddle attachment (or a big bowl using a handheld mixer), beat the butter and the sugar on low speed until combined. With the mixer running, add the eggs one at a time, letting each one totally mix in before adding the next. Use a rubber spatula to scrape the sides and bottom of the bowl. Add the sour cream, ginger, cinnamon, salt, almond extract, baking powder, and baking soda and mix on low for 1 minute more, until everything is combined. Set a small mesh strainer over the bowl, pour in the flour, and tap to sift over the batter. Mix on low for 1 more minute, then scrape the sides and bottom of the bowl again.

Scrape the batter over the peaches. Slide the pan into the oven and set a timer for 30 minutes. (If you're using a 9-inch cake pan, set the timer for 25 minutes.) Slide a toothpick into the center of the cake. If it comes out clean or with a few crumbs, you're good. If not, set a timer for 5 minutes and test again.

*Recipe continues*

Set a timer for 15 minutes to let the cake cool slightly. Use oven mitts or thick kitchen towels to protect your hands. Put the cake pan in one hand and set the serving plate on top, making sure it's centered. Put your other hand on top of the plate and quickly flip. If the cake doesn't drop onto the plate (it's going to, but I just want to be sure), set the plate on the counter and lightly tap once or twice. The parchment will probably come out with the cake, but if it stays in the pan and holds any peach slices captive, just pluck them out and place them back in their slot on the cake. Let the cake cool for about 30 minutes before serving, or cool completely. Serve the slices plain, with whipped cream, or with ice cream.

## PARTY TRICKS

- For pitting instructions, see Party Tricks on page 221. This can also be done with a 16-ounce bag of frozen sliced peaches that has been thawed in the fridge overnight.

- If you're traveling with this cake, strategically stick toothpicks between a few of the peach slices, then loosely cover the plate with plastic wrap so it's tented on the toothpicks.

- Any leftover cake can be covered and refrigerated for up to 5 days.

# Flourless Chocolate Olive Oil Cake

IN YOUR SLEEP | V, GF, NF

For over a decade, this has been my signature dessert, and it's one of the things I repeatedly get asked to bring by name. Part of me wants to gatekeep, but it's just so good. Plus (do me a favor, keep this between us), it's the easiest cake you're ever going to make. Like boxed cake level of unbelievably simple, but bakery level of unbelievably chic. I can't wait for you to know the joy of drolly sighing about your signature dessert.

**Makes a 9-inch cake**

1 (4-ounce) semisweet or bittersweet chocolate bar
¾ cup (150 grams) sugar
½ cup (40 grams) cocoa powder
½ cup (120 grams) extra-virgin olive oil
1 navel orange
1 teaspoon freshly ground black pepper
½ teaspoon kosher salt
3 large eggs
Powdered sugar and Maple Whipped Cream (page 207), for serving (both optional)

**SPECIAL EQUIPMENT**
9-inch (or 8-inch) springform pan

Preheat the oven to 350°F and set a rack in the center. Lay a large piece of parchment over the base of a 9-inch (or 8-inch) springform pan, then set the springform ring on the base and snap it into place. Do not grease the pan or parchment. I like the rustic look of the flowing parchment in the final presentation, but you can trim it to the edge of the pan if you want. Set the pan on a rimmed baking sheet for safety's sake.

Set the chocolate bar on a large cutting board and use a serrated knife to cut diagonally across the bar. Rotate the cutting board a quarter turn and cut diagonally in the other direction to create small pieces. Melt the chocolate (see Party Trick). Scrape the chocolate into a medium bowl.

Add the sugar, cocoa powder, and olive oil and whisk until completely combined. Zest the orange directly into the bowl, then add the pepper and salt and whisk again. Let the mixture cool for about 5 minutes before cracking the eggs into the bowl. Whisk until the eggs are fully incorporated.

Scrape the batter into the prepared pan and wiggle once or twice to smooth the top. Slide the cake into the oven and set a timer for 35 minutes. (If you're using an 8-inch pan, set the timer for 40 minutes.) The cake will be gooey, so insert a toothpick just to make sure there's no raw batter in the center. Add 5 more minutes to the timer if it needs it. Cool for 15 minutes, then run a butter knife around the perimeter of the cake to make sure the edges don't stick to the pan. Unlatch the springform but keep it around the cake while it finishes cooling, about 2 hours.

*Recipe continues*

I like to serve the cake on the base with a skirt of parchment, but you can run an offset spatula under the cake to release and transfer to a platter. Either dust the cake with powdered sugar before serving or whip up a bowl of maple whipped cream to serve alongside for dolloping, or live a little and do both.

## PARTY TRICKS

- Scrape the chocolate into a small microwave-safe bowl. Microwave at full power in 15-second intervals, stopping to stir with a rubber spatula after each one. When the chocolate is 75 percent melted, probably 45 to 60 seconds, let the residual heat take care of the rest, then stir once more. To do this on the stove, fill a small saucepan with 1 inch of water and bring to a simmer over medium heat. Scrape the chocolate into a medium bowl and set over the saucepan, making sure the bowl doesn't touch the water at all. Let the heat slowly melt the chocolate, using a spatula to slide the unmelted chocolate into the center. When the chocolate is 75 percent melted, remove from the saucepan and let the residual heat finish the job.

- To transport the cake, relatch the springform around the cooled cake and wrap the entire pan in plastic. Bring any accoutrements with you.

- Leftover cake can be covered and refrigerated for up to 3 days.

# Birthday Suit Cake

ROLL UP YOUR SLEEVES | VG, NF (GF)

*Optional: Start this recipe 1 day ahead.*

Years ago, I was in upstate New York at my friend Mark Wier's house for his birthday. He wanted a Funfetti cake (king behavior) and I made one, but I seriously underestimated the amount of frosting I would need to coat two layers. So I served this naked cake instead, with frosting piled in the middle and on top, and completely exposed sides. I thought it was so cute to see a cake in its birthday suit, and crumb coatings are annoying anyway, so now it's the only way I do Funfetti.

**Makes a two-layer 8-inch cake**

Nonstick cooking spray

CAKE

1 cup (2 sticks) unsalted butter, at room temperature (see Party Tricks)

2 cups (280 grams) all-purpose flour or gluten-free flour (see Party Trick on page 215)

1½ cups (300 grams) granulated sugar

¼ cup cornstarch (30 grams)

2 teaspoons baking powder

1 teaspoon kosher salt

3 large egg whites

2 tablespoons pure vanilla extract

¼ cup (60 grams) vegetable oil

1 cup plus 1 tablespoon (245 grams) whole milk

¾ cup (140 g) rainbow sprinkles (see Party Tricks)

**Make the cake:** Preheat the oven to 350°F and set a rack in the center. Set two 8-inch (or 9-inch) cake pans right-side up on a big piece of parchment. Trace around the bottoms of the pans, then cut around the inside of the circles to avoid the ink. Coat the bottom and sides of the pans with nonstick spray, press the parchment rounds to the bottom, and spray again.

In the bowl of a stand mixer fitted with the paddle attachment (or a big bowl using a handheld mixer), beat the softened butter with the flour, granulated sugar, milk powder, baking powder, and salt on low to combine into a crumbly mixture. (See Party Tricks.) Add the egg whites one at a time, letting each one totally mix in before adding the next, then add the vanilla. Remove the bowl from the mixer and scrape down the sides and bottom of the bowl.

In a liquid measuring cup, pour in vegetable oil to hit the ¼ cup line, then pour in the milk until it hits the 1¼-cup line. Give it a good whisk to mix all together. (If you're being a perfect angel and working by weight, just do this in something with a pour spout.) Return to low speed and slowly pour in the milk mixture. Once the liquid is mixed in, crank it up to medium speed just for 1 minute to aerate the batter. Scrape down the sides and bottom again, then fold in the sprinkles by hand.

Evenly divide the batter between the prepared cake pans. (See Party Tricks.) Slide the pans into the oven and set a timer for 25 minutes. (If you're using a 9-inch cake pan, set the timer for 20 minutes.) Slide a toothpick into the center of each cake. If it comes out clean or with a few crumbs, you're good. If not, set a timer for 5 minutes and test again. Let the finished cakes cool completely in the pan, about 2 hours. (And before you step away, set out the butter to soften for the frosting!)

*Ingredients and recipe continue*

## FROSTING

½ cup (1 stick) unsalted butter, at room temperature

1 (8-ounce) block cream cheese, cut into cubes and chilled

3 cups (360 grams) powdered sugar

2 teaspoons pure vanilla extract

¼ cup (45 grams) rainbow sprinkles, plus more for garnish

Store-bought or homemade ice cream (page 179), for serving (optional)

**When the cakes are cool, make the frosting:** Wash and dry your paddle attachment and mixer bowl and click both back onto the stand mixer (or grab your clean handheld mixer again). Whip the softened butter, powdered sugar, and vanilla on low to combine, then crank up to medium-high to aerate the mixture, about 2 minutes. Stop and use a rubber spatula to scrape the sides and bottom of the bowl. Scatter the cream cheese cubes in. Mix on low until combined, then mix on medium-high for 1 more minute to make a super-fluffy frosting. Remove the bowl from the mixer and use the spatula to fold in the sprinkles. Refrigerate the frosting for 15 minutes before spreading.

Set one cake layer on a large cutting board and saw a serrated knife across the top to trim any domed top off. On a cake platter or serving plate, use the spatula to place a little blob of frosting dead center. Flip the cake layer upside down and center on the platter. Use the spatula to scoop about half of the frosting on top of the cake and spread in an even layer right to the edge. Coat the frosting with a few generous pinches of sprinkles. Trim the second layer, flip upside down, and center over the base, making sure the edges line up. Spread the rest of the frosting on top, this time leaving about ½-inch border around the edge and flicking some waves over the surface. Coat with a good layer of sprinkles again.

Serve with ice cream or let the cake be a solo act, it's up to you. Just pop in birthday candles and you're ready to go!

## PARTY TRICKS

- If you're like me and you're never going to remember to set your butter out, here's what you do: Stand your sticks (in their wrappers) vertically in the microwave. Microwave for 5 seconds, flip them to the other side, 5 seconds, flip. Keep going, giving them a little squeeze each time, until they're softened.

- I've tried every sprinkle under the sun and only one that will stop your Funfetti from looking like a summer camp tie-dye: Betty Crocker Parlor Perfect Crunchy Rainbow Sprinkles. A 9-ounce container will be plenty to get the job done.

- When you need to divide anything, weigh your empty bowl before you start. When your mixture is done, weigh the bowl, subtract the bowl weight, and divide what's left by 2 (or whatever division you need).

- If you want to start this recipe a day early, see Party Tricks on page 212.

- Any leftover cake can be covered and refrigerated for up to 5 days.

# Brown Sugar Angel

**BRAGGING RIGHTS | VG, NF**

A perfectly spongy angel food cake is, to me, exactly what summer is all about. It's just light enough to not be overly filling, it's the perfect amount of sweet, and it's basically engineered to soak up syrupy, fresh fruit. To make it even more angelic, I swap in brown sugar for a light caramel flavor and pleasantly tan hue. The sweetness has a little more body and the cake is even more spongy from the molasses in the sugar. I'll be real: making an angel food cake is an exercise in technique and patience. So don't be discouraged if there are a few flops at first! Once you get a feel for the whites and the batter, you'll be churning these out all summer.

**Make one large cake that serves 10 to 12**

1 cup packed (215 grams) dark brown sugar
⅔ cup (135 grams) granulated sugar
1 tablespoon cornstarch
1 cup (120 grams) cake flour (see Party Tricks)
12 large egg whites (see Party Tricks)
1½ teaspoons cream of tartar
¼ teaspoon kosher salt
1 teaspoon vanilla extract
Pepper Strawberries (recipe follows) or Maple Whipped Cream (recipe follows), for serving (optional)

**SPECIAL EQUIPMENT**
12-cup tube pan with removable bottom (see Party Tricks)
Stand mixer

Preheat the oven to 350°F and set a rack in the lower third. Do not grease the tube pan at all; the cake will only work if it can cling to the sides.

In a food processor, zip the brown sugar, granulated sugar, and cornstarch for 2 minutes until it's a fine powder. Tap about half of the sugar (175 grams) into a small bowl. Add the flour to the food processor with the other half of the sugar and zip again until they're mixed and very light, about 1 minute. Unclick the processor bowl from the machine and take the blade out for easy pouring later.

Make sure your stand mixer bowl is completely clean and completely dry before starting; any lingering fat is the enemy of egg whites. Use the whisk attachment to beat the egg whites on medium speed until they're frothy, about 1 minute. Add the cream of tartar and salt and increase to medium-high. With the mixer running, hold the small bowl over the whites and very slowly tap in the reserved sugar. Add the vanilla too. Continue beating until the whites are soft, glossy, and filling the bowl, 5 to 6 minutes (see Party Tricks).

Remove the bowl from the mixer. Lay a piece of parchment next to the bowl and set a medium mesh strainer on the parchment. Scoop about half of the flour-sugar mixture into the strainer, then tap the strainer to sift onto the parchment. Hold the strainer over the bowl, fold the parchment to pour in the flour mixture, then tap to sift a second time over the egg whites. Use a rubber spatula to very slowly and gently fold, getting all the way to the bottom and turning the bowl after every fold. When that's almost incorporated, repeat the double sift with the rest of the flour mixture. Fold until completely combined, but don't overmix.

Use the spatula to scoop blobs of the batter around the pan, then smooth the top into an even layer. Very lightly lift and tap the baking sheet twice to help the batter settle. Slide onto the lower rack and set a timer for 20 minutes. Reduce the oven temperature to 325°F and set the timer for 20 more minutes.

*Recipe continues*

Don't you dare open that oven door until the second timer goes off! (Except in an emergency situation, of course.) The cake should be golden brown and cracked on the top. Slide a toothpick deep into one of the cracks to test. If it comes out clean or with a few small crumbs, you're good. If not, set the timer for 5 more minutes, then test again. Flip the finished cake upside down so it's resting on the pan's feet and cool completely, 3 to 4 hours.

Flip the cake back over. Slide a thin knife with a long blade along the side of the pan. Hold the knife in place, pressing the blade firmly against the pan, and use your other hand to rotate the pan. Slide the knife in the center, pressing against the tube, and rotate the pan again. Lift the cake out by the tube, then slide the knife under the cake, pressing against the base, and use the tube to turn the cake. Set a platter on top of the tube and quickly flip to release the cake. It can be served immediately with berries and cream, or covered loosely with plastic wrap and stored at room temperature overnight.

### PARTY TRICKS

- Swans Down and Softasilk are my preferred cake flour brands for a pillowy soft cake. (King Arthur makes a good one too!) Unfortunately, all-purpose flour and/or any hacky transformations of all-purpose into cake flour just won't work; it's too dense and it deflates the whites.

- I've tested several brands of egg white cartons because I love a cheeky shortcut, but unfortunately the heavy pasteurization of carton whites gets in the way of a fluffy cake. There's no avoiding it—you'll have to manually separate a dozen eggs. The egg yolks can be refrigerated in airtight containers for up to 3 days and used to make a couple batches of ice cream (page 179)!

- Tube pans are sometimes sold as angel food cake pans, but don't confuse them with Bundt pans, which won't work here. Look for a pan that has feet around the edge, or an elongated center tube, to rest the cake upside down.

- To test the whites, stop the mixer and unclick the whisk. Dip the whisk in the whites, lift it out, and flip upside down. If the whites are runny, keep whisking. If the mixture makes a semi-firm peak that droops to the side, you're good.

- If you're traveling with this cake, keep it loosely covered with plastic wrap until you get there and bring any accoutrements along.

- Leftover cake can be covered and left at room temperature for up to 3 days.

# Pepper Strawberries

IN YOUR SLEEP | V, GF, NF

Black pepper and strawberries do not seem like natural bedfellows, but the lightly citrusy, piney heat of a freshly cracked peppercorn is actually the best possible partner.

**Makes 2 cups**

1 pound strawberries
2 tablespoons sugar
¼ teaspoon kosher salt
Freshly ground black pepper

Wash the strawberries under cold water. Slice the stems off, then cut the strawberries in quarters (or halves for smaller guys). In a large bowl, toss the strawberries with the sugar and salt, then cover with a kitchen towel to let sit at room temperature for 1 hour or cover with plastic wrap to refrigerate overnight. When it's time for them to make their entrance, set a pepper grinder to the biggest, coarsest grind and really go for it. You want at least 1 tablespoon, which is more than you think it is, but I usually get closer to 2 tablespoons. Stir the pepper in and serve right away.

# Maple Whipped Cream

IN YOUR SLEEP | VG, GF, NF

This whipped cream has minerally maple syrup and tart sour cream mixed in. But I think of it as the perfect subtly tangy-sweet support to pretty much any cake or pie that needs a little dollop of something. Just promise me you won't break my heart and use something that starts with Aunt, Log, or Mrs. This is worth buying the real stuff.

**Makes 2 cups**

1 cup (230 grams) very cold
  heavy cream
¼ cup (60 grams) sour cream
¼ cup (80 grams) pure maple
  syrup

In a medium bowl, combine the cream, sour cream, and maple syrup. Use a large whisk to beat vigorously until the cream doubles in size and makes a stiff peak when you lift the whisk out and flip it over, about 7 minutes. This can also be done with a handheld mixer on low speed for about 4 minutes. The whipped cream can be served right away or refrigerated in an airtight container for up to 8 hours.

# Burnt Cheesecake

IN YOUR SLEEP | VG, NF

*Optional: Start this recipe 1 day ahead.*

When so many countries all over the world have a signature version of cheesecake, it says everything you need to know about how stellar cheesecake is. I love them all, but if I had to pick one it would be a Basque-style burnt cheesecake. It's by far the most forgiving version—No crust! You burn it on purpose!—and the deeply caramelized sugars in its signature dark exterior give it such a rich flavor, it hardly needs any accompaniment.

## Makes a 9-inch cake

4 (8-ounce) blocks full-fat cream cheese, at room temperature
2 cups (400 grams) sugar
4 large eggs
1½ cups (350 grams) heavy cream
6 tablespoons (50 grams) all-purpose flour
1 tablespoon pure vanilla extract
½ teaspoon kosher salt
1 navel orange
Pepper Strawberries (page 207) or Maple Whipped Cream (page 207), for serving (optional)

### SPECIAL EQUIPMENT
9-inch (or 8-inch) springform pan

## PARTY TRICK

• Leftover cake can be covered and refrigerated for up to 3 days.

**Two hours before you start,** pull the cream cheese out of the fridge to soften.

Preheat the oven to 400°F and set a rack in the center. Take two 14-inch pieces of parchment, crumple them into a tight ball, then smooth them out. Completely cover the bottom and sides of a 9-inch (or 8-inch) springform pan with the parchment, letting it pop out over the top. Do not grease the parchment—it'll stop the cake from rising. Set the cake pan on a rimmed baking sheet.

In the bowl of a stand mixer fitted with the paddle attachment (or in a big bowl using a handheld mixer), beat the cream cheese and sugar on low speed until combined. With the mixer running, add the eggs one at a time, letting each one totally mix in before adding the next. Beat on high for 5 minutes, until the mixture is airy and light. Use a rubber spatula to scrape the sides and bottom of the bowl. Add the cream, flour, vanilla, and salt to the bowl and then zest the orange directly into the bowl. Mix on low for 1 minute more, until everything is combined, then run the spatula around the bowl again.

Scrape the batter into the prepared pan. Slide it into the oven and set a timer for 60 minutes. Resist the urge to open the oven door for at least 50 minutes so the cake can properly rise. When the cake is done it'll be dark brown and set on the surface, but still a little jiggly when you wiggle the baking sheet. Give it another 5 minutes if it needs it and check again.

Cool in the pan for 2 hours. The cake will deflate quite a bit, but don't panic. At this point you can unlatch and remove the springform, then peel the parchment away and serve in a rustic parchment blanket. Or you can fold the parchment over the top of the springform, wrap the entire pan in plastic, and refrigerate overnight. Remove from the fridge at least 2 hours before serving. Serve the slices solo, with pepper strawberries, or maple whipped cream.

# Bruce Bogtrotter Cake

IN YOUR SLEEP/ROLL UP YOUR SLEEVES/BRAGGING RIGHTS | VG, NF

*Optional: Start this recipe 1 day ahead.*

If you get this reference, we are family. For the uninitiated, Bruce Bogtrotter is a character in the Roald Dahl book—and, more important, the Danny DeVito–directed cinematic masterpiece—*Matilda*. After Bruce sneaks a piece of Miss Trunchbull's chocolate cake, she makes him eat an entire cake in front of the whole school. And let me tell you, that gorgeous, moist, layered, frosted chocolate cake leapt off the screen and seared itself into my brain for all eternity. So here it is, my dream chocolate cake, in honor of Brucey. The number of layers and amount of effort is up to you—one is perfect for a snacking cake, two is beautiful and impressive, three is a supreme act for someone you really love.

---

**Makes an 8-inch cake, as many layers as you want**

Nonstick cooking spray

**SINGLE-LAYER CAKE**
½ cup (40 grams) unsweetened cocoa powder
½ cup (115 grams) hot coffee
½ cup (130 grams) cold buttermilk
¼ cup (60 grams) vegetable oil
1 cup (200 grams) sugar
1 large egg
1 teaspoon pure vanilla extract
1 teaspoon baking soda
½ teaspoon baking powder
½ teaspoon kosher salt
1 cup (140 grams) all-purpose flour

---

**Make the cake:** Preheat the oven to 350°F and set a rack in the center. Set an 8-inch (or 9-inch) cake pan right-side up on a piece of parchment. Trace around the bottom of the pan, then cut around the inside of the circle to avoid the ink. Coat the bottom and sides of the pan with nonstick spray, press the parchment round to the bottom, and spray again.

In a large bowl, whisk the cocoa powder and coffee together. Let it sit for 5 minutes so the cocoa flavor can bloom, then whisk in the buttermilk. Whisk in the vegetable oil and sugar, then the egg and vanilla until the egg is completely mixed in. Whisk in the baking soda, baking powder, and salt. Set a small mesh strainer over the bowl, pour in the flour, and tap to sift over the batter. Use a rubber spatula to fold in the flour until it's just mixed.

Scrape the batter into the prepared pan (see Party Tricks) and give it a wiggle to smooth the top. Slide the pan into the oven and set a timer for 40 minutes. (If you're using a 9-inch cake pan, set the timer for 35 minutes.) Slide a toothpick into the center of the cake. If it comes out clean or with a few crumbs, you're good. If not, set a timer for 5 minutes and test again. Let the finished cake cool completely in the pan, about 2 hours. (Before you take a break, set out the butter to soften for the frosting!)

**When the cake is cool, make the frosting:** Melt the chocolate (see Party Tricks on page 199). Give the melted chocolate 10 minutes to cool before continuing with the frosting.

In a large bowl, use a handheld mixer (or a stand mixer with the whisk) to beat the softened butter and cooled chocolate together on low to combine, then

*Ingredients and recipe continue*

## FROSTING FOR A SINGLE LAYER

1 (4-ounce) semisweet or bittersweet chocolate bar, chopped

½ cup (1 stick) unsalted butter, at room temperature (to soften quickly, see Party Tricks on page 202)

2 cups (240 grams) powdered sugar

¼ cup (60 grams) sour cream

1 tablespoon heavy cream or whole milk

1 tablespoon light corn syrup (it's fine, see Party Tricks on page 180)

½ teaspoon pure vanilla extract

¼ teaspoon kosher salt

crank up to medium-high to aerate the mixture, about 2 minutes. Stop and use a rubber spatula to scrape the sides and bottom of the bowl. Add the powdered sugar, sour cream, heavy cream, corn syrup, vanilla, and salt, then mix on low until combined. Go back to medium-high for 1 more minute to make a super fluffy frosting. Refrigerate the frosting for 15 minutes before spreading.

Flip the cooled cake out of the pan and discard the parchment. Set it facing up on a large cutting board and saw a serrated knife across the top to trim the dome off. On a serving plate or cake platter, use the spatula to place a little blob of frosting dead center. Flip the cake upside down and center on the platter. Rip four strips of parchment paper and slide them just under the cake so you can frost without making a mess. Use a regular or offset spatula to scoop about half of the frosting on top of the cake and spread in an even layer to the edge. Scoop a small amount of frosting onto the spatula and spread a thick vertical stripe on the side of the cake. Rotate the plate as you continue to frost the side a little at a time. Any extra frosting can be used to even out the sides and top. Slide the parchment strips out, lick off the frosting, and discard. You're ready to serve!

## PARTY TRICKS

- If you're making more than one layer, see Party Tricks on page 202 for an easy way to divide the batter.

- If you're making two layers, double the cake and frosting recipes. Bake the cakes and divide the frosting evenly between two small bowls. Trim and set one cake layer with parchment. From one bowl, use half of the frosting on top and another half around the side. Trim the second layer and set upside down on top of the base, then use half of the remaining frosting on the side and the last of the frosting to smooth on top. For three layers, triple the recipes, divide the frosting among three bowls, and follow the same process. For four layers, buy cake skewers and pray.

- If you want to start this recipe a day early, transfer the frosting to an airtight container and refrigerate overnight, then let it sit at room temperature for 30 minutes before spreading. Wrap the cooled cakes tightly in plastic and let sit at room temperature overnight. If you're traveling with this cake, you can either assemble and frost at home or trim the cake top(s) and wrap up tight again, and bring all the pieces with you to assemble there.

- Leftover cake can be covered and refrigerated for up to 5 days.

# Gluten-Free Loaf Cake

IN YOUR SLEEP | GF

Every other cake in this chapter was developed with wheat flour, with a gluten-free swap where I could. But for all my gluten-free friends and allies, I wanted something in this chapter to start from a gluten-free mindset. The flavor options run from approachable (Apple + Rose, mmm!) to exciting (Banana + Espresso) to revolutionary (Ketchup + Spice). I felt your sharp inhale at that last one, so let me just say it's A) my favorite of the three and B) the secret ingredient none of my friends could guess. The ketchup gives a very slight tang and a sort of savory background that makes a really complex spice cake. But all three are beautiful, moist loaves ready for you to bake.

**Makes one 9-inch loaf**

Nonstick spray
Demerara sugar
1 cup (200 grams) granulated
   sugar
¼ cup (60 grams) vegetable oil
2 large eggs
1 teaspoon kosher salt
1½ teaspoons baking powder
Flavorings (see chart below)
1½ cups (210 grams) gluten-
   free flour (see Party Tricks)
1 cup (100 grams) almond flour

**SPECIAL EQUIPMENT**
9 by 5-inch loaf pan

Preheat the oven to 325°F and set a rack in the center. Coat a 9 by 5-inch loaf pan with nonstick spray, then generously sprinkle in Demerara sugar and tap it so it sticks on all sides, tipping out any extra. (This is a good project to do over the sink.) Set the pan on a rimmed baking sheet to be safe.

In a large bowl, whisk the granulated sugar, vegetable oil, and eggs together with some muscle until it's all looking fluffy, about 2 minutes. Add the salt, baking powder, baking soda, and flavorings and whisk again. Add the gluten-free flour and almond flour and use a rubber spatula to stir. (No need to worry about overmixing here, there's no gluten!) Set a timer for 5 minutes so the flour can hydrate. Scrape into the prepared baking pan, give it a wiggle to distribute, and sprinkle a little more Demerara over the top.

Slide the baking sheet into the oven and set a timer for 60 minutes, but do a check-in around 50 minutes to be safe. When a toothpick inserted in the center comes out clean or with a few crumbs, you're good. Otherwise, keep baking for 5 more minutes and check again. Cool completely in the loaf pan, about 2 hours. The loaf should release easily, but you can run a butter knife around the edge if it's stuck anywhere.

| FLAVORINGS | |
|---|---|
| **APPLE + ROSE** | 1 cup (270 grams) apple butter and 2 tablespoons rose water |
| **BANANA + ESPRESSO** | 1 cup mashed banana (from 2 very ripe bananas) and 2 tablespoons espresso powder |
| **KETCHUP + SPICE** | 1 cup (265 grams) ketchup and 2 tablespoons pumpkin pie spice |

## PARTY TRICKS

- My favorite gluten-free flours are King Arthur's Measure for Measure and Bob's Red Mill 1 to 1 Baking Flour, but any brand that includes xanthan gum will work. Remember, gluten-free flour hydrates differently than wheat flour, so always let the batter sit for 5 minutes before transferring it to a pan.

- To transport the cake, cover the cooled pan with plastic wrap until you get there.

- Leftover cake can be covered and stored at room temperature for up to 3 days.

CRISPY
SAUCE!

PLUM + WALN

HOT FUDGE

BREAD OIL

PRESENT
MOMENT

**I AM PHYSICALLY INCAPABLE OF** showing up empty-handed. If you say "Just bring yourself," my brain goes into overdrive for a perfect gift. I'm cataloging your apartment: Have I ever seen a plant that's not on life support, are you more of an incense or candle person, is your coffee table stacked with pretty books you've definitely never read, and so on. But what I've learned over and over is A) the best gifts are always homemade and B) food never fails. So for all of us who can't just bring ourselves, this chapter has a few perfect solutions that will always hit the mark.

# Bread Dipping Oil

IN YOUR SLEEP | V, GF, NF

Warm bread and a plate of really good oil. Are you crying? I'm crying. This oil is quickly infused with the entire Simon & Garfunkel song, plus one secret ingredient: miso paste. It sneaks in undetected but adds a ton of salty, savory flavor to the oil that boosts everything around it. If you're really feeling it and want to bake some warm homemade bread to go with it, wow, I love you, can you come to my house?

## Makes 2 cups

2 cups grapeseed oil (see Party
  Tricks)
1 bunch chives
6 parsley sprigs (stems are
  fine)
8 thyme sprigs (stems are fine)
Leaves from 1 sage sprig
Leaves from 2 rosemary sprigs
Leaves from 4 basil sprigs
1 tablespoon white miso paste
1 tablespoon fennel seeds
1 tablespoon whole black
  peppercorns
2 teaspoons dried oregano
½ teaspoon garlic powder
½ teaspoon red pepper flakes

### SPECIAL EQUIPMENT
Two 8-ounce squeeze bottles

Before you start, make sure the squeeze bottles and lids you're about to use are thoroughly scrubbed with soap and hot water. (If you need to run the dishwasher anyway, throw them in there and come back to this page when they're done.)

Set a medium mesh strainer over a large measuring cup or a heatproof bowl with a pour spout. Nestle a coffee filter or cheesecloth in the strainer.

In a blender, combine the grapeseed oil with the chives, thyme, parsley, basil, sage, rosemary, white miso, fennel seeds, black peppercorns, dried oregano, garlic powder, and red pepper flakes. Blend on low until everything is broken up but not totally smooth, about 1 minute.

Pour the mixture into a medium saucepan and set over the lowest possible heat. Stir occasionally until the mixture starts sizzling, about 8 minutes. Remove from the stove and pour into the coffee filter to strain. Let gravity do its job (meaning don't stir or press) so the oil comes out nice and clear.

Pour the oil into bottles, seal, and let sit somewhere cool and dark until you're ready to hand them out, which should be in the next day or two.

### PARTY TRICK

- I know, it's tempting to use your best olive oil here. But listen to me: Do. not. do. it. The minute that oil touches the blades of a blender, it'll turn bitter and no amount of herbs are going to save you. "Then don't blend it!" you scream. But blending the herbs demolishes their cell walls for insane flavor. I love your bond with olive oil so much, but you're just going to have to trust me here.

# Plum + Walnut Jam

ROLL UP YOUR SLEEVES | V, GF (NF)

More than a decade ago, my friend Henry Lyon's mom made me a jar of plum and walnut jam and I would say, conservatively, I've thought about that moment once a week ever since. There is no act more tender than making a jar of jam for someone. Make sure the plums are ripe—they can be so bitter before they're sweet—but still a little firm for max pectin content. The walnuts are what make this jam really special, but you can totally leave them out if you need to make it nut-free.

**Makes two ½-pint jars, plus a little extra for you**

2 pounds ripe plums, pitted (see Party Trick)
1½ cups sugar
2 tablespoons fresh lemon juice (from 1 lemon)
¼ teaspoon kosher salt
1 cup roughly chopped raw walnuts

SPECIAL EQUIPMENT
Two ½-pint jars
Candy or deep-fry thermometer (optional)

Before you start, save yourself from bacteria and make sure the jars and lids you're about to use are thoroughly scrubbed with soap and hot water. (If you need to run the dishwasher anyway, throw them in there and get it started. They'll be ready by the time you need them.)

Cut the plums into 1-inch-thick slices. In a large saucepan, combine the plums, sugar, lemon juice, and salt. Use your hands to quickly toss everything together, then cover the saucepan and set a timer for 2 hours to let the fruit macerate. Go take a break.

When the timer goes off, take a minute to toast the walnuts. In a small skillet, arrange them in an even layer. Set over medium heat, tossing or stirring occasionally. Use your knuckles to carefully press on the tops of the walnuts; when they feel hot, usually 3 to 4 minutes, remove the skillet from the stove and set aside to cool.

Put on an apron, just in case this gets messy. Remove the lid from the saucepan and attach a thermometer if you have one. If you don't, put a small plate in the refrigerator for later. Place the saucepan over medium heat and set a timer for 30 minutes, more to mark time than as an exact science. Stir occasionally as the fruit starts to soften and the juices start to boil. Once it really gets going, around 10 minutes in, stir constantly to make sure the plums don't scorch. If you're following along on your thermometer, continue to stir constantly for another 15 to 20 minutes until it hits 220°F, then remove from the stove.

If you're flying without a thermometer, this paragraph is for you: After another 15 to 20 minutes of constant stirring, the fruit will be broken down, the liquid will mostly evaporate, and the jam will be thick with big bubbles like lava. Trust your eyes more than the timer on this one. When you hit the lava stage, remove the saucepan from the stove. Grab that cold plate from the fridge, spoon a little bit of jam in the center, then put it back in the fridge for 2 minutes. Once it cools, quickly run your finger through the jam. If you make a clean line and both sides of the jam stay put, you're golden. If not, put the plate back in the fridge, put the saucepan back over medium heat, and set the timer for 5 more minutes before trying again.

When the jam is ready, stir in the toasted walnuts. Use a soup spoon to fill two ½-pint jars, leaving about ¼ inch of space at the top, and twist the caps on tight. Place the jars in the refrigerator to cool, at least 2 hours or overnight. Any bonus jam is yours and it can be enjoyed right away on toast or refrigerated in a small (clean!) airtight container and enjoyed within a day or two.

Rip off a piece of tape for each jar and use a Sharpie to write what this is (it's Plum + Walnut Jam, in case you forgot) and a use-by date exactly two weeks from today (you're on your own for that one). Gift one or both jars right away so that person has the maximum amount of time to enjoy it!

## PARTY TRICK

- To pit the plums—and this works for any stone fruit—hold the fruit in one hand and a paring knife in the other. If the stem is the North Pole, cut all the way around the fruit from north to south, then turn the fruit in your hand to keep cutting around the equator. Twist the top and bottom in opposite directions and you'll be able to pop the pit out and slice the fruit.

# Homemade Hot Fudge

ROLL UP YOUR SLEEVES | VG, GF, NF

Having a little jar of hot fudge winking at you from the fridge is beyond compare, and anyone you give this to will feel the same way. When I make a batch just for me, it's not uncommon to find me dipping a spoon in real quick just to make sure it's still good and maybe one (three) more spoonful to confirm. It thickens in the fridge, but under a gentle heat it melts into the ideal balance of thick-runny, perfect for drizzling over any and every dessert.

**Makes 1 pint jar, plus a little extra for you**

1 (4-ounce) semisweet or bittersweet chocolate bar
4 tablespoons unsalted butter
1¼ cups sugar
⅓ cup cocoa powder (see Party Tricks)
½ teaspoon kosher salt
½ cup whole milk
½ cup heavy cream
1 tablespoon light corn syrup (relax, see Party Tricks on page 180)
1 teaspoon pure vanilla extract

**SPECIAL EQUIPMENT**
One 1-pint jar

## PARTY TRICK

- I prefer the taste of Dutch-processed cocoa powder here, which could be as simple as Hershey's Special Dark 100% cocoa, or something more luxe like Droste or Valrhona. If you already have a box of regular cocoa powder around, just use that.

Before you start, save yourself from bacteria and make sure the 1-pint jar and lid you're about to use is thoroughly scrubbed with soap and hot water. (If you need to run the dishwasher anyway, throw it in there and come back to this page when it's done.)

Use a serrated knife to cut diagonally across the chocolate bar. Rotate the cutting board a quarter turn and cut diagonally in the other direction to create small pieces. Slide the chocolate to one side. On the other side, cut the butter in half lengthwise, then cut across in 4 equal pieces. Keep everything close by, we'll need them in a moment.

In a medium saucepan, whisk the sugar, cocoa powder, and salt together until the cocoa is no longer lumpy. Pour in the milk and cream. Whisk again—and I mean whisk!—until the cocoa mixture is fully hydrated. Cocoa powder will burn and get bitter easily, so put your biceps in it. I'd really encourage grabbing a spatula and running it around the edges and bottom just to be sure.

Set over low heat and continue whisking occasionally. When sugar melts and the sauce is runny, about 5 minutes in, remove from the stove. Add the chopped chocolate and let it sit for 5 minutes to slowly melt. Add the butter, corn syrup, and vanilla, and give the sauce a good whisk until the chocolate and butter are fully incorporated.

Pour the sauce into the jar, leaving about ¼ inch of space at the top, and twist the cap on tight. Place the jar in the refrigerator to cool, at least 2 hours or overnight. Any bonus hot fudge is yours and it can be enjoyed right away on ice cream or refrigerated in a small (clean!) airtight container and enjoyed within a couple days.

Rip off a piece of tape for the jar and write what this is (it's Homemade Hot Fudge, silly goose) and a use-by date exactly two weeks from today (ask a calendar if you're not sure). Be a good friend and gift the jar as soon as you can!

# Crispy Sauce

BRAGGING RIGHTS | V, GF, NF

I used to make hot sauce for a living, so it's safe to say I'm obsessed with all things spicy. Top of my list is a savory, tingly, sweet chili crisp, but there's always been a little voice in my head that wanted to find a way to pack all that flavor into a squeezable sauce. Crispy Sauce (and there really is no other appropriate name) starts as a chili crisp and then gets tangled up with a few untraditional ingredients for an extremely flavorful hot sauce. It's all my wildest dreams come true, and a perfect gift for every hot sauce lover in your life.

## Makes 2 cups

1 cup grapeseed oil
2 scallions, cut into 1-inch pieces
1 medium shallot, thinly sliced
1 (1-inch) piece fresh ginger, peeled and thinly sliced
2 garlic cloves, thinly sliced
1 cinnamon stick
6 cardamom pods
6 whole cloves
4 star anise pods
2 tablespoons Sichuan peppercorns
1 tablespoon fennel seeds
2 tablespoons chile flakes (see Party Trick)
1 tablespoon sugar
1 tablespoon white miso paste
1 tablespoon tomato paste
1 tablespoon mayonnaise, vegan or not
1 tablespoon rice vinegar
1 packet Sazón seasoning, either saffron or coriander and annatto flavor (see Party Tricks on page 90)

**SPECIAL EQUIPMENT**
One 8-ounce squeeze bottle

Make sure your squeeze bottle and lid are thoroughly scrubbed with soap and hot water. (If you need to run the dishwasher anyway, throw it in there and get it started. It'll be ready by the time you need them.)

In a medium saucepan, combine the oil, scallions, shallot, ginger, and garlic. In a spice grinder—or clean coffee grinder or zip-top bag with weaponized rolling pin—combine the cinnamon, cardamom, cloves, star anise, Sichuan peppercorns, and fennel seeds. Pulse (or whack) a few times to roughly crush them, then add to the oil. Set the saucepan over low heat and set a timer for 15 minutes, just as a guide. Stir occasionally and when the shallots are deep golden brown all over (trust your eyes over the timer) remove from the heat and stir in the chile flakes. Cover and set a timer for 2 hours to cool completely.

Set a small mesh strainer over a liquid measuring cup and strain the oil until you end up with around ½ cup. Press hard with the spatula to get the last bits of flavor before discarding the spices. In a stand mixer fitted with the whisk attachment—or a big bowl using a handheld mixer—combine the sugar, miso paste, tomato paste, mayo, vinegar, and Sazón. Start blending on low, then increase the speed to high. Drizzle the oil in an excruciatingly slow stream until it's all whipped into an emulsified sauce.

Set a funnel in the bottle and pour the sauce through. Rip off a piece of tape for the bottle and write what this is (it's Crispy Sauce, hello) and a use-by date exactly 1 month from today (that's an easy one). Refrigerate the bottles until you're ready to hand them out, which is ideally as soon as possible.

## PARTY TRICK

- My favorite for this sauce is erjingtiao, a spicy Sichuan chile that is floral and fragrant. Alts are earthy and umami Aleppo pepper from Syria and sweet and smoky gochugaru from Korea. All three are easily available online or in specialty stores. (Common red pepper flakes won't work here.)

# Seasoned Oyster Crackers

IN YOUR SLEEP | V, NF

**My mom and I used to make seasoned oyster crackers every year to give to our friends at Christmastime. They're impossibly easy to make (and impossibly hard to stop snacking on), but just because they're simple doesn't mean they're any less special. First of all, oyster crackers are in my top tier of crackers—they're so adorable and perfect for eating by the handful, which is not true of all crackers. They also have a singular flavor profile (salty) that really lets you paint whatever picture you want. I have three spice blends spelled out for you—Sweety + Salty, Herby + Spicy, Tingly + Smoky—but whatever is already in your spice rack is going to make perfect sense here. My mom and I would bake a big batch to divide among cello bags printed with holly vines, blue snowflakes, or other '90s ideas of tasteful, then tie on colorful ribbons. And you know who was especially touched to receive our little gifts? EVERYONE!**

**Makes 5½ cups**

4 tablespoons unsalted butter,
  vegan or dairy
1 (9-ounce) bag oyster
  crackers
Seasonings (see chart
  opposite)

**SPECIAL EQUIPMENT**
Comically large bowl
Cello bags, mini brown bags, or
  small airtight containers

Preheat the oven to 250°F and set a rack in the center.

In a small saucepan, slowly melt the butter over low heat. When it's about 50 percent melted, remove it from the stove to finish melting on its own. (A microwave and a bowl is also an option, just let it cool for a couple minutes.)

Set a colander in the sink and pour in the bag of crackers. (This has to be a colander with holes big enough to let the crumbs through; otherwise just shake the cracker bag vertically so the crumbs fall to the bottom.) Shake the colander up and down to let the crumbs fall to the bottom and crackers rise to the top. Keep shaking until you feel like almost all the crumbs are out.

Wash your hands or put on food service gloves. Use your hands to scoop the crackers into a comically large bowl (trust me, you'll want plenty of room to toss) and leave the last of the crumbs in the colander. In a small bowl, pinch the seasonings together. Pour the butter over the crackers and toss with your hands. Sprinkle in half of the seasonings, toss, then the other half, and toss again.

Spread the crackers out on a naked rimmed baking sheet and slide it into the oven. Set a timer for 15 minutes. Pull the baking sheet out, stir the crackers, maybe shake the sheet to move them all around, then return to the oven. Set a timer for 10 minutes. They should be nicely golden brown by now; if not, give them 5 more minutes.

Let the crackers cool completely on the baking sheet, about 1 hour, then transfer to cello bags. (Or an airtight container if you're keeping these for yourself.) Seal the bags tightly and maybe tying on a little tag with the flavor profile wouldn't be a bad idea. The crackers should be enjoyed within one week which, in my experience, has never been a problem.

## SEASONINGS

| | |
|---|---|
| **SWEETY + SALTY** | Stir 2 tablespoons honey (or agave) into the melted butter. (Dip the tablespoon into the melted butter before squeezing the honey and it'll slide right out!)<br><br>Mix together 4 teaspoons nori flakes, 2 teaspoons demerara sugar, 2 teaspoons flaky sea salt, and an optional ½ teaspoon togarashi for heat. |
| **HERBY + SPICY** | Mix together 2 teaspoons dried thyme, 1 teaspoon dried rosemary, 1 teaspoon dried oregano, 1 teaspoon red pepper flakes, 1 teaspoon mustard powder, and ½ teaspoon kosher salt. |
| **TINGLY + SMOKY** | Pulse 1 teaspoon Sichuan peppercorns in a (clean!) coffee grinder, spice grinder, Nutribullet, or throw them in a bag and whack them with a rolling pin or meat tenderizer until they're crushed.<br><br>Mix together the peppercorns, ½ teaspoon smoked salt, ½ teaspoon smoked paprika, and an optional ½ teaspoon chipotle powder for extra heat. |

# THE FULL RECIPE LIST

**V = Vegan**
**VG = Vegetarian**
**GF = Gluten-Free**
**NF = Nut-Free**
**NA = Nonalcoholic**

## Breads and Crackers

# ON A SCALE OF LOW-KEY TO SHOWY

## In Your Sleep (Super Easy)

33   White Beans + Tinned Fish *GF, NF*
35   Salt + Vinegar Salsa Verde *V, GF, NF*
36   Muhammara *V, GF*
43   Whipped Blue Cheese *VG, GF, NF*
47   Spiced Hibiscus Punch *V, GF, NF, NA*
48   Whole Lemon Lemonade *V, GF, NF, NA*
53   Surfer on Acid *V, GF*
58   Pitcher-Perfect Margaritas *V, GF, NF*
61   Staycation *V, GF, NF*
64   Amaro Hot Chocolate *VG, GF, NF (NA)*
74   Herb Salad with Homemade Ranch *VG, GF, NF*
89   Maple-Miso Smashed Cucumbers *V, GF, NF*
90   Black Bean Salad with Sazón Vinaigrette *V, GF, NF*
95   Dirty Horchata *VG, GF, NF, NA*
100   A Triflin' Parfait *VG, NF (V, GF)*
111   Radish + Seaweed Butter *V, GF, NF*
123   Cornmeal Crackers *VG, NF (GF)*
130   Cheese Twists *VG, NF (GF)*
133   Blender Cornbread *VG, NF (GF)*
140   Scrunchy Bread *VG, NF*
156   Mango + Sticky Rice Pudding *V, GF, NF*
163   Milk + Cookies *VG, NF (GF)*
168   Party Krispies *NF (GF)*
169   Blackberry + Basil Pie *VG, NF (V, GF)*
193   Easy Apple Cake *VG, NF*
197   Flourless Chocolate Olive Oil Cake *VG, GF, NF*
208   Burnt Cheesecake *VG, NF*
211   Bruce Bogtrotter Cake *VG, NF*
214   Gluten-Free Loaf Cake *GF*
219   Bread Dipping Oil *V, GF, NF*
224   Seasoned Oyster Crackers *V, NF*

## Roll Up Your Sleeves (Some Effort)

23   Golden Ratio Guac *V, GF, NF*
27   Faux Gras *V, GF (NA)*
28   Seven-Onion Dip *VG, GF, NF (V)*
30   Silky Hummus *V, GF, NF*
39   Pico de Sandia *V, GF, NF*
40   Vegan Elote Queso *V, GF, NF*

50   Arnie Palmer *V, GF, NF, NA*
54   Picklebacks *V, GF, NF*
57   Jell-O Cocktail Shots *GF, NF*
69   Caesar Salad with Bouillon Crouton *VG, GF, NF*
73   Pickled Potato Salad *VG, GF, NF (V)*
77   Shrimp Cocktail Ceviche *GF, NF*
78   Fried Halloumi Caprese *VG, GF, NF*
81   Perfect Pasta Salad *VG, NF*
85   Waldorf Salad with Poppy Dressing *VG, GF*
86   Bagel Panzanella *V, GF, NF*
96   Orange Cantaloupe Agua Fresca *V, GF, NF, NA*
99   The Best Bloody *GF, NF (V, NA)*
107   Loaded Rösti *GF, NF (V, VG)*
112   Gochujang + Cheddar Scones *VG, NF*
115   Cheesy Breakfast Tart *VG, NF*
124   Herby Challah *VG, NF*
127   Potato Parker House Rolls *VG, NF*
134   Fluffy Pitas *V, NF*
137   Seeded Barbari *V, NF*
143   Dreamy Focaccia *V, NF*
146   Parmesan Round *VG, NF (GF)*
151   Mosaic Jell-O *GF, NF*
155   Buttermilk Brownies *VG, NF*
164   Apple + Chinese Five-Spice Pie *VG, NF (V, GF)*
171   Subway Cookies *VG (GF)*
179   Very Creamy Ice Cream *VG, GF, NF*
185   Lemon Bar Cake *VG, NF*
189   Pumpkin Carrot Cake *VG (NF)*
194   Peach + Ginger Upside-Down Cake *VG, NF (GF)*
200   Birthday Suit Cake *VG, NF (GF)*
220   Plum + Walnut Jam *V, GF (NF)*
222   Homemade Hot Fudge *VG, GF, NF*

## Bragging Rights (Extra Focus)

62   Hazelnut Eggnog *VG, GF (NF)*
103   Cream-Soaked Cinnamon Rolls *VG, NF*
116   Box of Donuts *VG, NF*
175   Raspberry Meringue Tart *NF (GF)*
205   Brown Sugar Angel *VG, NF*
223   Crispy Sauce *V, GF, NF*

# ACKNOWLEDGMENTS

My name is on the cover, but a lot of people made this book happen.

My mom, **Sue Elsass**, thank you for teaching me to always be curious, imaginative, and expansive when thinking about food.

My boyfriend, **Pacifico Silano**, an endless source of laughs, inspiration, taste tests, kitchen concerts, and head rubs. Your love makes me feel unstoppable.

My agent, **Alison Fargis**, who is my biggest cheerleader and best sounding board. Thank you for doing the hard work so I can do the fun work. Everything feels possible with you in my corner.

My editor, **Caitlin Leffel**. From the moment we met, I felt you understood this book inside out and backward, and that feeling has never changed. Thank you for supporting, nurturing, and improving our book every step of the way.

My photographers, **Andrea Gentl and Martin Hyers**. Thank you for the limitless positivity, flexibility, and creativity. My food stylist, **Tyna Hoang**, for doing the impossible and making it seem effortless. My prop stylist, **Stephanie De Luca**, for elevating every shot to the best possible place. Watching you four work was the greatest gift of this entire process. And to the army of support, including **Joyce Mills**, **Frankie Crichton**, **Coco Hill**, **Lucy Reback**, **Adeline Hume**, **Andrea Nguyen**, and **Loz McInnes**, who made this shoot come to life.

My most trusted palates, **Ben Weiner**, **Jacqui Tris**, **John deBary**, **Sam Burros**, and **Zoe Denenberg**, who picked these recipes apart and put them through their paces. And my favorite minds on this planet, **Amanda Odmark**, **Chris Benecke**, **Sam Neuman**, and **Taylor Griggs**, who untangled scraps of ideas, marked up finished drafts, and shut down stupid jokes.

The best friend of the century, **Jason Hudson**, who was there for me every step of the way, including driving down from Canada to be the glue that held the shoot together. And **Emily DePaula** and **Robbie Guevarra**, my two favorite food brains, who logged hours on the phone, listening to my endless stream of "but what if . . ." as I put together a puzzle of recipes.

Thank you to the entire Union Square team, including **Lisa Forde**, **Linda Liang**, **Ivy McFadden**, **Terence Campo**, and **Terry Deal**, for turning my Word doc into a real book, and especially **Renée Bollier**, who spun my silly little ideas into a beautiful design. And to **Amanda Englander**, thank you for bringing me into this world in the first place and teaching me everything I know about writing a cookbook.

An enormous thank you to all the friends whose arms, legs, hands, and torsos made the photos come alive: **Andre Springer**, **Angela Krasnick**, **Ayesha Nurdjaja**, **Dan Pelosi**, **David Bertozzi**, **David Sabshon**, **Deb Perelman**, **Edy Massih**, **Elizabeth Svokos**, **Farideh Sadeghin**, **Jeremy Bennett**, **Jeremy Salamon**, **Jessie Sheehan**, **Justine Doiron**, **Lindsay Ratowsky**, **Marsha Drummond**, **Merik Goma**, **Michael Herman**, **Mo Fayaz**, **Oscar Nuñez**, **Patrick Janelle**, **Renato Poliafito**, **Samantha Seneviratne**, **Sarah Carey**, **Srishti Jain**, **Stephanie Francis**, **Taylor Miller**, **Todd Heim**, **Vardaan Arora**, **Vicky Chen**, **Vivian Bond**, and **Woldy Kusina**. Your collective love and enthusiasm is what makes this book so special.

I can hear the orchestra playing me off, but I want to quickly thank the editorial and culinary teams at *Bon Appétit*, **BuzzFeed**, **Delish**, and **Food Network** for sharpening me as a cook and a writer. And finally, a big thank you to the **Brooklyn Public Library** for an incredible collection of cookbooks and food media, and especially the Bushwick Branch for being my quiet working space when I got antsy in my apartment. Librarians are the angels of every community. Support your local library!

# INDEX

NOTE: Page references in *italics* refer to photos of recipes.